SCHOLASTIC INC., 2931 East McCarty Street, Jefferson City, MO 65102
Or call (800) 325-6149 between 7:30 a.m. and 5 p.m. Central Time. In Missouri, call (800) 392-2179.

INSTRUCTOR RESOURCE SERIES

Big Idea Book — 750 best classroom do-its and use-its from Instructor magazine. 49000.
Big Basics Book — 55 master plans for teaching the basics, with over 100 reproducibles. 49001.
Big Holiday Book — Seasonal songs, stories, poems, plays, and art, plus an activities calendar. 49002.
Big Seasonal Arts & Crafts Book — Over 300 projects for special days and seasons. 49003.
Big Language Arts Book for Primary Grades — 136 reading and language skills reproducibles. 49004.
Big Math Book for Primary Grades — 135 reproducibles on number concepts and processes. 49005.
Big Book of Teacher Savers — Class lists, letters to parents, record-keeping forms, calendars, maps, writing forms, and more. 49006.
Synonyms, Sentences, and Spelling Bees: Language Skills Book A — 140 reproducibles. 49007.
Periods, Paragraphs, and Prepositions: Language Skills Book B — Over 140 reproducibles. 49008.
Big Book of Reading Ideas — Teacher-tested reading ideas for use with any reading system. 49009.
Teacher's Activity Calendar — Red letter days, ideas, units for the school year. 49010.
Early Education Almanac — Hundreds of activities for kindergarten and beyond. 49011.
Paper, Pen, and Think — Ideas galore for developing a sequential writing program. 49012.
Beating the Bulletin Board Blues — Step-by-step ways to bulletin board learning centers. 49013.
Success with Sticky Subjects — Books A and B together offer over 240 reproducible worksheets for classroom drill in problem areas of the curriculum. **Book A** — 49014 **Book B** — 49015.
Foolproof, Failsafe Seasonal Science — Units, experiments, and quick activities. 49016.
Poetry Place Anthology — 605 favorite poems from Instructor, organized for instant access. 49017.
Big Book of Plays — 82 original, reproducible plays for all occasions and levels. 49018.
Artfully Easy! — "How-to" workshops on teaching art basics, group projects, and more! 49019.
Big Book of Study Skills — Techniques and activities for the basic subject areas. 49020.
Big Book of Study Skills Reproducibles — Over 125 classroom-tested worksheets for all levels. 49021.
Big Book of Computer Activities — A hands-on guide for using computers in every subject. 49022.
Read-Aloud Anthology — 98 stories for all grades and all occasions. 49023.
Page-a-Day Pursuits — Over 300 reproducibles on famous days, birthdays, and events. 49024.
Big Book of Holiday Word Puzzles — 400 skill-builders for 130 year 'round celebrations. 49025.
Big Book of Health and Safety — Reproducible activities to shape up the health curriculum. 49026.
Teacher Savers Two — Reproducible awards, contracts, letters, sanity-keepers galore. 49027.
Celebrate America — Over 200 reproducible activities about the symbols, the land, the people of the U.S.A. Maps, graphs, timelines, folklore, and more. Eight pull-out posters. 49028.
Big Book of Absolutely Everything — 1001 ideas to take you through the school year. 49029.
Language Unlimited — 160 reproducibles sharpen reading, writing, speaking, listening skills. 49030.
Children and Media — Activities help kids learn from TV, radio, film, videotape, print. 49031.
Blockbuster Bulletin Boards — 366 teacher originals for all grades, subjects, and seasons. 49032.
Hey Gang! Let's Put On A Show — 50 original skits, choral readings, plays for all ages. 49033.
Puzzle Pals — Mazes, decoders, wordsearches, hidden objects and more. 49034.
Hands-On Science — Jam-packed with facts and activities to develop young scientists, K-8. 49035.
21st Century Discipline — Practical strategies to teach students responsibility and self-control. 49036.
Learning to Teach — A blend of research on teaching with the practical insights of experienced teachers. 49037.
Loving Literature — Literature selections and accompanying activities that encourage kids to laugh, cry, wonder, and keep on reading. 49038.
Teaching Kids to Care — 156 activities to help young children cooperate, share, and learn together. 49039.
Games, Giggles, and Giant Steps — 250 games for children ages 2-8; no equipment needed. 49040.
Everybody Sing and Dance — 80 hands-on, shoes-off song, dance, rhythm, and creative movement experiences. 49041.
Toward Tomorrow — Reproducible activities that challenge students to focus on and believe in the future. 49070.

Scholastic Inc. grants teachers permission to photocopy the activity sheets from this book for classroom use. No other part of this publication may be reproduced in whole or in part, or stored in a retrieval system, or transmitted in any form or by any means, electronic, mechanical, photocopying, recording, or otherwise, without written permission of the publisher. For information regarding permission, write to Scholastic Inc., 730 Broadway, New York, NY 10003.

ISBN 0-590-49024-9
Copyright © 1984 by Instructor Books. This edition published by Scholastic Inc. All rights reserved.
12 11 10 9 8 7 6 5 4 3 2 1   9/8 0 1 2 3 4/9
Printed in the U.S.A.
First Scholastic printing, February 1990

Acknowledgements:
This book is written by Rosemary Alexander, with editorial assistance from Susan Gaustad. Cynthia Amrine is art director and designer. Patty Briles is illustrator, with research assistance from Christopher Briles. Production coordinators are Elisa Chavez, Judy Cohn, and Debi Harmer.

August 21

Name _____

A Basketball Record Breaker

Wilt Chamberlain, born in 1936, has been called the greatest basketball player of all time. He has the record for the most points in a regular season, highest average points per game, and most free throws in a game. In fact, most of the National Basketball Association records were made by this man. Probably his biggest success came in 1962, when he made 36 field goals and 28 free throws to score 100 points in a single game. No one else has ever come close to that record!

Wilt has an interesting nickname. Solve these problems. Then write the letter that's beside each problem in the space above the correct answer below. When the problems are solved, the letters will spell out his nickname. Is it an appropriate one for a person over seven feet tall?

```
36 field goals        80 games                12,681 field goals
x2                    x50 points a game       x2
T                     T                       T


31,419 total points         I             63 points
-25,362 free throws      2)48 points       -9
         E                                   H


      L                    72 field goals
80)4,000 points          +28 free throws
                                S
```

__ __ __
4,000 54 6,057

__ __ __ __ __
100 25,362 24 50 72

7

August 22

Name_____

A First Air Race

Airplanes were not yet six years old when the First International Air Race was held in Rheims, France, in 1909. The winner was an American named Glenn Curtiss, who finished the 20-kilometer course in 15 minutes and 50.6 seconds, or 75.75 kilometers per hour.

Have your own air race. Follow these diagrams to make a paper airplane, then see how far it will fly. When you make the folds, be sure to crease them firmly with a pencil or other object. Ask your teacher if you can use the school hall or gym for your air field.

1 Take a sheet of paper about 8½" x 11".

2 Fold in half lengthwise.

3 Open paper up, with fold going up and down, and fold corners A and B down, so they touch center fold.

4 Now fold each half again toward the center, so that corners C and D touch center fold.

5 Fold paper in half.

6 Fold each wing in half outward, towad the top fold, so point E touches point F.

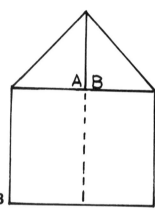

7 Now turn airplane over, hold at bottom fold, and it's ready to fly!

August 23

Name _____

Flying By Man Power

For many years a prize of 50,000 British pounds had been offered to anyone who created a machine that could fly on man power alone. It seemed as if no one would ever win, but finally in 1977 Bryon Allen flew a 70-pound machine around a one-mile route by using foot pedals. The machine looked like a bicycle on wings. And that's not all. Two years later he pedaled a similar machine for 22 miles across the English Channel to help win an even larger prize.

The two machines were called the *Gossamer Condor* and the *Gossamer Albatross*. Look up these words in a dictionary or an encyclopedia and write their definitions.

gossamer _____

condor _____

albatross _____

Were these good names for the machines? Why or why not? _____

August 24

Name_____

Liberian Flag Day

Liberia is a small country in Africa. It was created by black people from the United States who moved there in 1822. Liberia is close to the United States in many ways.

Its capital is called Monrovia in honor of James Monroe, who was president of the United States in 1822.

The government is organized very much like ours.

Its flag resembles the American flag.

Liberia uses U.S. money as its currency.

Look at a classroom map of Africa, then draw Liberia on this map. Mark and label its capital.

Color this Liberian flag. Remember, it has the U.S. flag colors.

August 25

Name_____

A Fast Bike Ride

How fast can you go on your bike? How about 140½ miles per hour? In 1973 Dr. Allan Abott went that fast, but only under special conditions. He raced on very flat, hard ground and was protected by a windshield on the back of a car moving ahead of him. For most people, even a speed of 40 miles an hour is too hard to reach.

Do you know your bike safety rules? How many things can you think of that you should always keep in mind when riding a bike? Here are some to get you started.

1. Ride your bike in the same direction as the traffic is going.
2. Signal with your hand when making a turn.
3. Wear something white or reflective at night.

4. _____

5. _____

6. _____

August 26

Name_____

Televised Baseball

Baseball fans were really excited on this day in 1939. For the first time they could see a major league ball game without going to the stadium. Viewers sat in their living rooms and watched a doubleheader between the Cincinnati Reds and the Brooklyn Dodgers, thanks to television.

All kinds of sports events are televised today. Check a television guide for last Saturday and Sunday.
    Write four sports events you could have watched.
    Put an X beside any you did watch.
    Put a ✔ beside any you wish you had seen.

_____

_____

_____

_____

What sport do you like to play? _____

Is it the kind of game you can watch on television? _____

August 27

Name_____

It's a Gusher

A driller struck oil in Pennsylvania in 1859. At first oil was only used to burn as fuel, to grease machinery, to put on roads, and to make kerosene for lamps. No one knew what to do with the gasoline left after making kerosene, so it was usually dumped in rivers to get rid of it.

Today hundreds of products are made from petroleum, another word for oil. Find some of them in this puzzle. Names are hidden across and up and down, both forward and backward.

A	P	K	O	H	R	J	E	S	P	P	B	W	Q
D	D	T	Z	N	S	M	G	D	L	L	F	R	U
E	V	B	K	I	O	U	J	R	S	A	C	E	A
T	I	V	A	C	F	B	K	J	H	S	A	P	R
E	G	A	S	O	L	I	N	E	F	T	G	A	X
R	C	U	P	S	E	R	I	T	N	I	A	P	E
G	L	N	H	L	D	G	X	F	H	C	E	X	O
E	M	Y	A	R	P	S	G	U	B	S	P	A	Y
N	N	Y	L	O	N	M	I	E	J	N	K	W	T
T	W	Y	T	B	O	T	T	L	E	D	G	A	S

    bug spray   tires   asphalt
    bottled gas   gasoline   jet fuel
    wax paper   ink   detergent
    paint   nylon   plastics

August 28

Name_____

Ready, Set, Go!

The starting gun went off! Sebastian Coe didn't hesitate. When the 1981 race was over, this young Englishman had set a new record—he had run a mile in 3 minutes and 47 seconds.

Pretend you are a sports announcer for your favorite TV or radio station. Prepare an account of this event to give on the 6:00 news. Help your listeners see Sebastian kneeling at the starting line, sprinting ahead at the gunshot, leaving other contestants behind, and whipping across the finish line. Think about what words to use. Will your voice be calm or excited?
   Practice the report by yourself, then announce it to the class or your family.

_____

_____

_____

_____

_____

_____

_____

_____

August 29

Name _____

How Did Chop Suey Get Its Name?

The Chinese chef had a problem. Here he was in New York City in 1896, looking for a food that both his employer, the Chinese ambassador to the United States, and the guests, including President Cleveland, would enjoy. He finally created a dish of chopped meat and vegetables and called his new food chop suey from two Chinese words—**shap** (miscellaneous) and **sui** (bits).

Many of our foods get their names in unusual ways. Read the definitions and descriptions below and match them with the correct foods.

____ Dessert to honor purchase of land from Russia.
____ It could be carried when traveling, so it was first called journey cake.
____ A butler in New Orleans named Praslin coated nuts with sugar to ward off indigestion.
____ When dogs began to howl at the smell of cooking fish, cooks tossed fried balls of the batter to quiet them.
____ When the molasses oozed to the top, it attracted flies that the cook chased away.
____ Beef soaked in vinegar and spices; its name from Germany means sweet and sour pot roast.
____ When a hotel opened in New York, the chef served a new salad.
____ This Spanish word means "little cake."
____ Its name is the county in Virginia where it was created.
____ Its original meaning is "framework of sticks."

1. Brunswick stew
2. hush puppies
3. tortilla
4. baked Alaska
5. barbecue
6. johnnycake
7. pralines
8. sauerbraten
9. Waldorf salad
10. shoo-fly pie

August 30

Name _____

Create a Monster

When Mary Wollstonecraft Shelley, who was born in 1797, and her husband moved to Italy, she began a book that would make her famous. *Frankenstein* is the story of a medical student named Victor Frankenstein who created a monster from parts of dead bodies. The monster was very gentle at first. But because it was ugly, people were unfriendly, and then it became savage and dangerous.

Cut out pictures of body parts from magazines and paste them here to make your own monster. You can make him or her beautiful or ugly, gentle or ferocious, depending on the pictures you use.

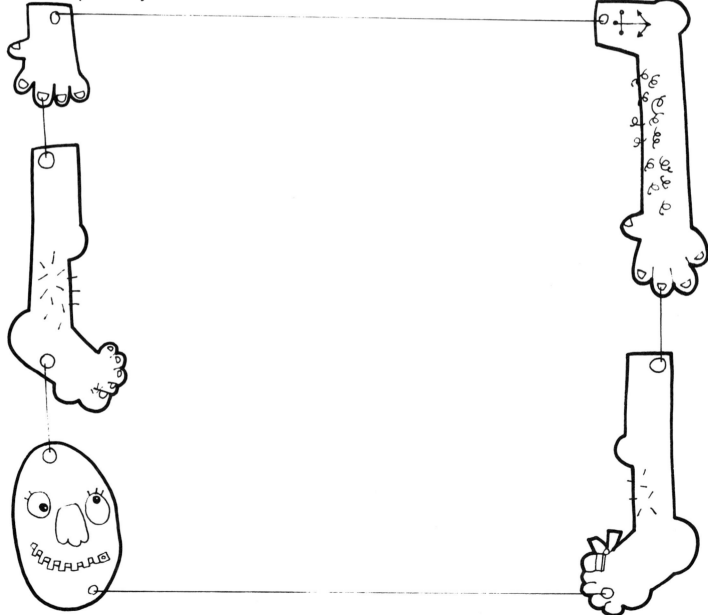

August 31

Name _____

Harness the Sun

In 1955 William Cobb made a model of a car that could be powered by the sun. His 15-inch "sunmobile" turned light into an electric current that drove a tiny electric motor. Cobb made it to show that there is unlimited power in the sun if we can learn to harness it.

You can use sun power to cook! First cut a six-inch cardboard circle. Cut a slit in it from the edge to the center, overlap the edges to make a cone, and tape to hold the shape. Line the inside with aluminum foil. Now put a piece of hot dog or a little hamburger at the bottom of the cone and prop the cone up in a place where the sun's rays hit it directly.

Check what time it is. Look at the cone in a half hour. Keep checking until your snack is done. You may have to adjust the cone so that it's always in the path of the sun's rays.

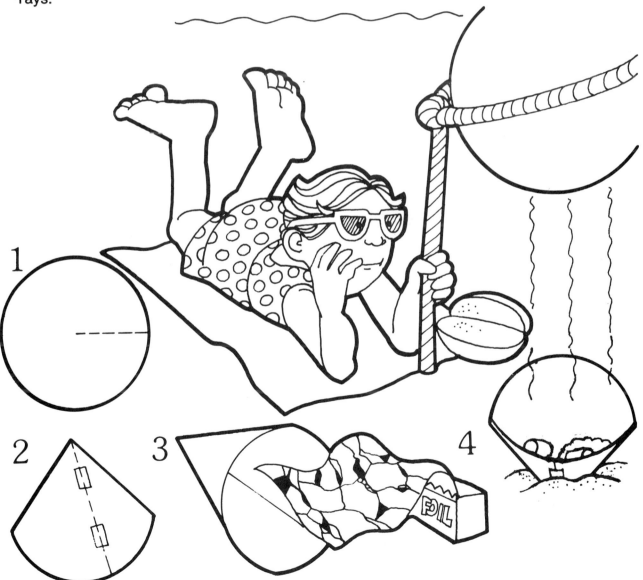

September 1

Name_____

Edgar Rice Burroughs

You may not know much about this man (born in 1875), but you are sure to know the hero of many of his books—Tarzan. Mr. Burroughs wrote his first Tarzan story in 1912. His first Tarzan book was published two years later. All together, he wrote 26 Tarzan books for boys and girls.

Visit your school or public library to see what Tarzan books it has. Write down the name of at least one here. Add more if you wish.

_____

_____

_____

Have you read any of them? Plan to start one this week.

September 2

Name_____

A New Calendar

People in England and its colonies went to bed on this date in 1752 and woke up on September 14. What happened? Why the missing 11 days? King George II decided to adopt a more accurate calendar, one that had been designed over 150 years earlier. It was called the Gregorian calendar and is the one we use today.

Pretend your birthday was on September 10 in 1752. Write a paragraph telling how you felt about losing a birthday and what you did to celebrate, even though the day had gone by. Did you ignore the new calendar, have an unbirthday party, pick a new day?

_____

_____

_____

_____

_____

September 3

Name_____

First Professional Football Game

On this day in 1895, a player was paid for playing football. The regular quarterback for the Latrobe, Pennsylvania, team could not play, so a substitute was hired for $10 plus his expenses. Two years later everyone on the team got paid for the games he played.

In honor of these early players, solve these math problems.

1. If the team had 20 players and each one was paid $10, how much money was spent for salaries at each game?

_____

2. If the team played 12 games in a season, how much did salaries cost for each season?

_____

3. Today players earn at least $60,000 a season. If a player plays 16 games, how much does he earn for one game?

_____

4. How much more does he earn than the first players did?

_____

5. Some star players may earn more than $60,000 a season, maybe 10 times as much. How much money is that?

_____

6. Write a problem of your own. Give it to a friend to solve.

_____

_____

September 4   Name _____

Extra, Extra!

Barney Flaherty didn't set out to be famous in 1833, when he was 10 years old. But we remember him as the first newspaper boy. He sold copies of the *New York Sun* for a penny each.

What paper is published in your town? _____

What does it cost? _____

How often is it published? _____

About how many pages does it usually have? _____

How does it get to your home? _____

Are there paper boys in your town? _____

Think about something that happened in your town this week. Write a headline about it as it might appear in your paper.

_____

September 5

Name_____

First Labor Day

Over a hundred years ago, a carpenter and a machine maker began to plan a special celebration to honor working people. The first Labor Day observance, a result of their plan, was a parade of 10,000 workers in New York City on this day in 1882. Today the United States and Canada celebrate Labor Day on the first Monday in September.

What date is the first Monday in September this year?_____

Many cities have special events on this day. In Mackinaw City, Michigan, for example, this is the only day in the year that people can walk the five miles across the Mackinac Bridge.

Tell about the Labor Day activities in your neighborhood. If there aren't any, describe a festival you'd like to have.

_____
_____
_____
_____

September 6

Name _____

Eat a Good Breakfast

Begin today to observe Better Breakfast Month by eating a good breakfast every day.

List four things that are good breakfast foods:

_____   _____

_____   _____

Paste pictures from magazines of some of these foods. Try to find pictures of your favorite ones. If you can't find them, try drawing them.

September 7   Name_____

Uncle Sam Is Born

Sam Wilson was an army meat inspector. His friends called him Uncle Sam. He stamped "U.S." on barrels of meat that passed inspection. On this day in 1813, Sam was mentioned in an article in a Troy, New York, newspaper. The article said that "U.S." stood for Uncle Sam as well as United States. The idea caught on and grew, and now the whole world recognizes Uncle Sam as the symbol for the country.

Many countries and groups are represented by symbols. How many do you know? Draw a line from each symbol to its correct group or country.

Russia
United States
Republican party
Canada
Christianity
Democratic party
Jewish religion

24

September 8

Name _____

Pledge to the Flag

The Pledge of Allegiance to the flag was published in *The Youth's Companion* magazine on September 8, 1892. It had been written by Francis Bellamy, an editor of the magazine. That same year school children recited it as they saluted the flag during a National School Celebration. This celebration was for the 400th anniversary of the discovery of America.

Here is the pledge as we know it today. Cut on the dotted line, design a red, white, and blue border, and take the pledge home to hang in your room.

I pledge allegiance to the flag

of the United States of America

and to the republic for which it stands,

one nation, under God, indivisible,

with liberty and justice for all.

September 9

Naming a Country

How would you like to pick a name for a country? That was the job of the Second Continental Congress in 1776. The men at this meeting needed to find a name for the 13 separate colonies that were working together to win their freedom from England. The winning name was United States of America.

If you were naming your country today, what might you call it? With a friend or the rest of the class, brainstorm names. List the most popular ones here.

_____

_____

_____

_____

_____

September 10

Name_____

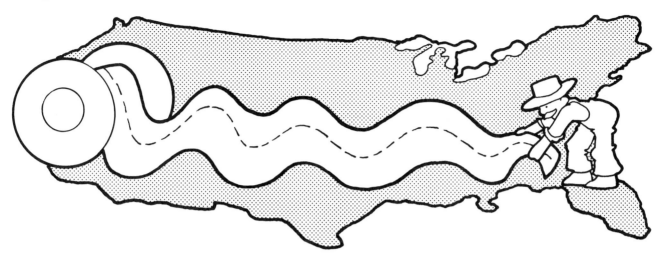

The Lincoln Highway

Plans for the first coast-to-coast paved highway were announced today in 1913. President Taft approved the idea, and the automobile manufacturers paid to have it built. It was called the Lincoln Highway. It is 3,385 miles long and goes through 13 states, from New York City to San Francisco. Today a large part of this road is U.S. Route 30.

Some things to think about.
1. What were most of the roads made of in 1913?

_____

2. Why would car makers want a good road?

_____

3. Who pays for our coast-to-coast roads today?

_____

4. What U.S. routes go through or near your neighborhood?

_____

5. When it was built, the Lincoln Highway was a two-lane road. How many lanes does the expressway or freeway nearest your home have?

_____

September 11

Name _____

A New Invention

In 1841 the toothpaste tube was invented. It was designed to hold paint but became more popular as a way to hold toothpaste. Many small but clever inventions make our lives simpler. Here is the start of a list of some of them. Add to it for a week. Compare lists with friends. Who can make the longest one?

1. toothpaste tube
2. clothespin
3. eraser on end of pencil
4. doorknob

5. _____ 8. _____

6. _____ 9. _____

7. _____ 10. _____

September 12

Name_____

Protect Your Eyes

September is Sight Saving Month, a time to think about some rules for good eye care. Always remember to keep sharp things away from eyes, wear goggles when nailing or sawing wood, and do not look directly into the sun.

Test your powers to see and observe. Look around the room. Can you see something that begins with each letter of the alphabet? How many of the blanks can you complete in five minutes?

a_____ n_____

b_____ o_____

c_____ p_____

d_____ q_____

e_____ r_____

f_____ s_____

g_____ t_____

h_____ u_____

i_____ v_____

j_____ w_____

k_____ x_____

l_____ y_____

m_____ z_____

September 13   Name_____

First Rhino in United States

In 1826 Americans got their first glimpse of a rhinoceros. Posters advertising it said, "Its body and limbs are covered with a skin so hard . . . that he fears neither the claws of the tiger nor the proboscis of the elephant; it will . . . even resist the force of a musket ball."

A rhino's skin is tough, but that poster was certainly an exaggeration. Do you know what "proboscis" means? If not, look it up in the dictionary. Think about a pet you have (or wish you had). Write two exaggerated sentences about it. Your description can make it seem ferocious, huge, strong, tiny, gentle, extremely talented, or whatever else you want.

_____

_____

_____

_____

You may want to make a poster to advertise your pet. Draw a picture of the animal and include your exaggerated description.

September 14

Name _____

A Song Is Born

What important U.S. song was written:
1. by a lawyer who wrote poetry as a hobby?
2. on an English battleship during a war?
3. to be sung to the tune of a drinking song?

Our national anthem! Francis Scott Key wrote it on this hazy morning in 1814. He was so happy when he saw our flag still flying after an all-night battle that he put his thoughts into words.

Every country has a national anthem. Here are the names of some of them. Can you match the songs with their countries?

Das Deutschlandlied	Japan
Himno Nacional de Mexico	England
O, Canada	Italy
God Save the King (Queen)	Federal Republic of Germany
Kimagayo	Canada
The March of the Volunteers	Brazil
Hinco Nacional	Mexico
Inno di Mameli	People's Republic of China

September 15

Name _____

Old People's Day

On this day the people of Japan honor their senior citizens. Help Japan celebrate by making a card to give or send to an older friend or relative.

Cut a piece of heavy paper about 5" x 8". Fold it in half. Draw and color an interesting picture on the front. Cut away the upper corner if you want to. Inside, write this verse or one you make up:

    Roses are red, violets are blue,
    Today is the day when I'm thinking of you.

  If there is a senior citizens' home nearby, your class might visit the residents and share with them the cards you've made. Tell them your name and something about yourself. Ask their names and give them a chance to tell you about their lives when they were your age.

September 16

Mayflower Day

On this day in 1620, 102 passengers left England in the ship *Mayflower* to start a new life in North America. No one really knows what the ship looked like, but experts think it was about 90 feet long and about 25 feet at its widest part. It had two decks. Measure its area on the playground. Do you think you and 101 other people could live there for over two months?

Pretend you are Richard or Ellen More, a brother and sister who were on the *Mayflower*. Write a paragraph about the trip. Tell where you slept, what you ate, what you did to keep amused. Remember, there were not enough bunks for everyone, not much room to run, and there could only be cooking fires on very calm days.

September 17

Name _____

Citizenship Day

This is a day to honor American citizens. What is a citizen? When you are born, you become a citizen (a native born citizen) of the country you were born in. People may give up a citizenship in one country to become citizens of another country. They are then called naturalized citizens. Each year several thousand persons become naturalized U.S. citizens.

Look at the graph below, then answer the questions.

	1 million	1¼ million	1½ million	1¾ million	2 million
1931-1940					
1941-1950					
1951-1960					
1961-1970					
1971-1979					

1. During what period did almost 2 million people become naturalized _____

2. How many people were naturalized from 1931 to 1940? _____

3. How many more people were naturalized from 1931 to 1940 than from 1971 to 1979? _____

4. In what period were the least number naturalized? _____

5. From 1931 to 1979, about how many persons became naturalized citizens of the United States? _____

September 18

Name _____

Something New to Play With

There was a new addition to toy departments in 1955. It was blue, yellow, and red, and was invented as a substitute for modeling clay. What was it? Play-Doh!

Create some nature creatures. First collect pebbles, shells, seeds, weed pods, or other things from outdoors. With Play-Doh, clay, or other material, model a body with short chubby legs. Then add your nature objects to make eyes, nose, mouth, ears, whiskers, and other features. Let your creation dry and use it for a paperweight.

If you want to make your own modeling material, take this recipe home and ask Mother to help. You will need:

- 1 cup sand
- ½ cup cornstarch
- ½ cup (or maybe a little more) boiling water

Have Mother help you cook this in a double boiler until it thickens. Use it to make your creature; then when it is molded, put it on a cookie sheet and bake in the oven at 275° F until dry.

September 19

Name_____

The Star of Steamboat Willie

A favorite cartoon creature was born today. When the cartoon film *Steamboat Willie* was first shown in 1928, its hero became an instant star. Today people around the world know and love Mickey Mouse.

Make paper-bag puppets of Mickey or Minnie Mouse. Stuff a paper bag and insert a wooden stick—it could be a piece of broom handle, a ruler, or any narrow wood strip. Tape the opening shut. Cut ears and nose from black paper. Glue in place. Paint on eyes and other features. Have a conversation with your puppet friend.

September 20

Name_____

National Courtesy Week

Remind yourself this week that courtesy is really a year-round activity and that it's important to be polite.

Add letters in the blanks below to complete six polite phrases we need to use every day.

PL _ A _ _

T_ _ N _ _ O _

_ _ U'R _ W _ L _ _ M _

M _ Y _ ?

I' _ _ OR _ _

_ _ LL _

With your friends, play a game that depends on being polite. Players line up side by side, about 40 feet (or any distance) from a goal line. "It" stands behind the goal line and says to each person, in turn, "Take a giant step (or a regular step, or a baby step)." That person asks, "May I?" "It" says, "Yes, you may," and the person takes the step. If the person forgets to say, "May I?" he or she loses the turn. First person to get to the goal line and touch "It" becomes the new "It."

37

September 21

Name _____

International Banana Festival

What do people do at a banana festival? If you live in Fulton, Kentucky, you probably eat part of a one-ton banana pudding. This huge dessert will serve the 10,000 people who come to the festival.

There is an old song about a fruit seller who never said no. One day he ran out of bananas. Soon someone came to buy bananas. Use this secret code to find out what the fruit peddler replied.

1-a	8-h	15-o	22-v
2-b	9-i	16-p	23-w
3-c	10-j	17-q	24-x
4-d	11-k	18-r	25-y
5-e	12-l	19-s	26-z
6-f	13-m	20-t	
7-g	14-n	21-u	

25 5 19,   23 5   8 1 22 5   14 15   2 1 14 1 14 1 19

___ ___ ___, ___ ___   ___ ___ ___ ___   ___ ___   ___ ___ ___ ___ ___ ___ ___!

Write a secret-code message describing the size of Fulton's banana pudding. Ask a friend to figure it out.

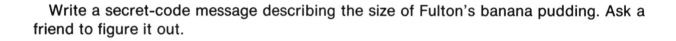

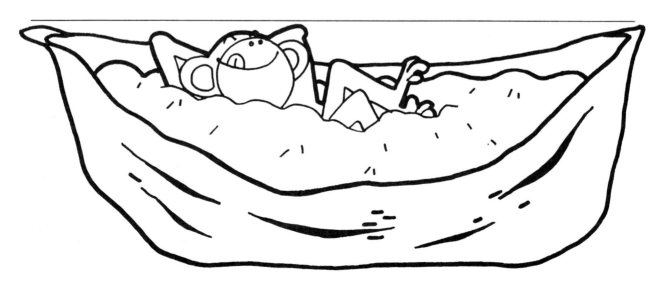

September 22   Name_____

A First Ice-Cream Cone

There are many stories about the invention of the ice-cream cone. One story says the owner of an ice-cream stand ran out of dishes, so he put ice cream into rolled-up waffles from the stand next door. This happened in 1904 at the Louisiana Purchase Exposition in St. Louis. Another story says the owner of ice-cream carts in New York City asked for a patent to make cones on this day in 1903. We're thankful to whomever the inventor was!

Boys and girls of long ago had a choice of only three ice-cream flavors. Unscramble these letters to find out what they were.

llaianv   leathococ   wreastyrbr

_____

Today we can get many flavors. Unscramble these letters to find six of them.

groane   nnbaaa   yrbrpeasr   thuccetbrots

_____

             rubett nacpe   tawlun

_____

What is your favorite ice cream?_____

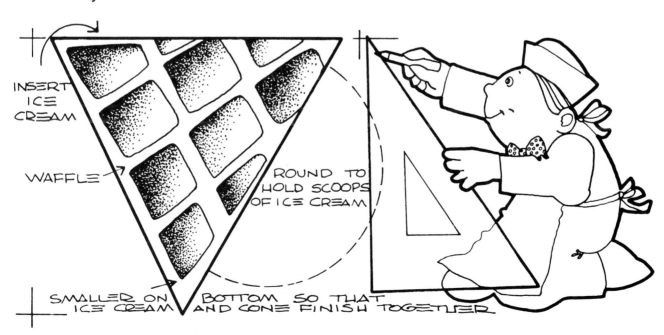

39

September 23

Name_____

Happy Birthday, Mr. McGuffey

Have you ever heard of William McGuffey, born in 1800? We should remember him because he helped millions of boys and girls learn to read. He wrote six reading books, one for each grade. On each page of these small books was a word list, a very short story, and a rule about an honest way to live. If your great-great-grandfather was a boy in the United States from about 1840 to 1900, he probably learned to read from *McGuffey's Eclectic Readers.*

Mr. McGuffey's first-grade book listed many word families. How large a family of words can you make from each of these roots? Add consonants or blends before each root to make words.

_ill	_at	_am	_in
____	____	____	____
____	____	____	____
____	____	____	____
____	____	____	____
____	____	____	____
____	____	____	____

September 24 Name _____

Honor Harry Behn

Today is the birthday of poet Harry Behn, born in 1898. This author liked nature and wrote many poems about it for boys and girls. A favorite one is "Trees." He called trees the kindest things he knew. He said they don't do any harm yet give us shade and fruit and wood; they sing a lullaby at night.

In his poem, Mr. Behn gave a human feeling to a plant. Try that yourself. We usually use the words here to describe people. But can you use each one to describe a plant, something in the weather, an animal, or a hill or mountain?

kind _____

angry _____

happy _____

friendly _____

wise _____

sad _____

You can find Mr. Behn's "Trees" in his book *The Little Hill*, and in other books of poems. The same book also has a poem about kites that would be fun to read on a windy day. Ask for it at the library.

September 25 Name_____

First Newspaper

The first newspaper in America was published this day in 1690 in Boston. It was called *Publick Occurrences Both Forreign and Domestick*. The governor of Massachusetts colony did not like what it said so this was the only issue. It was made of one sheet folded in half to form four pages. The last page was blank and there were no ads.

In memory of *Publick Occurrences*, make a collage of words to describe America. Cut the words from newspaper headlines and advertisements and arrange them on this page in an interesting design.

September 26   Name _____

Johnny Appleseed

John Chapman, born in 1774, spent most of his life growing apple trees. On his trips through the Ohio Valley, he often made gifts of apple seeds and sprouts to the settlers there. His neighbors began to call him Johnny Appleseed, and that is how we remember him.

Make apple prints in honor of Johnny. Cut an apple in half crosswise. It will look like this.

Let it dry for an hour or so. Press the apple onto a stamp pad or in very thick tempera paint and then press onto this page. Arrange apple prints in a pleasing design.

43

September 27

Name_____

Book Matches on the Way

In 1892 Joshua Pusey received a patent for making book matches. The covers of book matches have all kinds of designs. Some advertise a product, some show a beautiful scene. Sometimes people have them printed with their monograms. (A monogram is a person's initials arranged in a pleasing way.) Brides and grooms often give covers with their names and wedding date printed on them to wedding guests.

Design two matchbook covers. Make one that has your monogram. Plan the second one to advertise a new ball-point pen.

Many people collect matchbook covers as a hobby. Maybe you would like to start collecting them for *your* hobby.

September 28 — Name _____

Ask a Stupid Question Day

The people who thought up this day wanted to encourage curious people to ask any question they wanted to, no matter how silly. So put on your thinking cap and ask a question about something you wonder about.

Did you ever wonder how an elephant got a trunk, or why a leopard has spots? An English writer, Rudyard Kipling, wrote a book that gives humorous answers to questions like these. Ask your teacher to read parts of Kipling's *Just So Stories.* Or read them yourself.

   How do *you* think an elephant got its trunk? Write your reason here. Then compare it with Mr. Kipling's version.

_____

_____

_____

_____

September 29

Name_____

A Permanent Army

In 1789 the United States decided it should have a permanent army to protect the country. This first army had 700 men. Today the U.S. army has nearly 800,000 men and women. Besides working as soldiers, they also work as truck drivers, office workers, engineers, computer operators, musicians, and other professions.

When the army needs people, it displays posters to encourage men and women to join. This one is the most famous.

In the space here, design a poster telling about the army. Make it so interesting that people will want to join.

September 30

Name _____

First Fair in America

On this day in 1641, the government of New Netherlands ordered that there be fairs every year so people could exhibit and sell their products. Today every state has a state fair, and there are many county fairs. Sometimes city neighborhoods have street fairs. At fairs people exhibit foods, sewing projects, or animals. They watch contests. They enjoy special shows. They take carnival rides and try their hand at games of chance. They eat special foods.

Write a verse about some of the things you have seen at a fair. Start each line with these letters.

T _____

H _____

E _____

F _____

A _____

I _____

R _____

October 1

Name _____

Here Comes the Mailman

In 1896 three rural mail routes were started. Before that, people living in the country had to go to the post office in a nearby town to get mail. During the first week of the new rural routes, country residents received 214 letters, 290 papers, 33 postal cards, and 2 packages. They sent 18 letters and 2 packages.

Celebrate this day by sending a letter or postcard to a friend or relative who lives on a rural route. If you don't know anyone with a country address, write to a relative in another city. Be sure to tell why this is a special day.

October 2

Name_____

Phileas Fogg's Bet

Jules Verne was a French writer. He wrote science fiction stories about airplanes, submarines, and space satellites before they were even invented. In his book *Around the World in Eighty Days,* the hero is named Phileas Fogg. Mr. Fogg made a bet in London, at 8:45 P.M. on October 2, 1872, that he could complete a tour of the world in 80 days or less. He returned to London on December 21, with one second to spare, and won the bet.

Remember Phileas Fogg by seeing how many words you can make from the letters in his name. Make a bet with yourself that you can find at least 12 words in three minutes. After three minutes, can you find 12 more?

P H I L E A S   F O G G

Ask your teacher or a parent to read you some of Mr. Verne's tales. You'll especially like *Twenty Thousand Leagues Under the Sea* and *A Journey to the Center of the Earth.*

October 3

Name_____

Spectacle of the Geese

Each fall thousands of wild geese leave Canada to spend the winter in a warmer climate. Citizens of Fond du Lac, Wisconsin, watch as over 100,000 geese stop at a nearby swamp to rest and eat before going on. Wisconsin is on the Mississippi flyway. A flyway is a path birds follow when they migrate; there are four main flyways in North America.

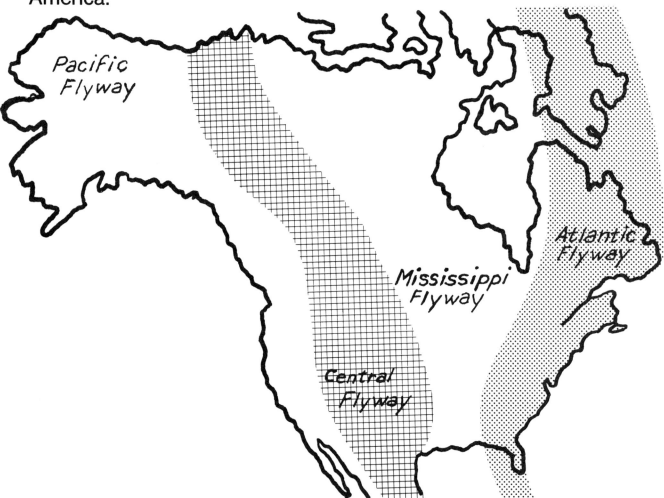

List six kinds of birds that live in your area. After each one put a Y if it is there year-round; S if it is there only in summer; W if it is there only in winter. Try to find out where one of these kinds of birds goes when it leaves your neighborhood.

October 4

Name_____

Launch of Sputnik I

The space age arrived in 1957 when the Soviet Union launched the first successful manmade earth satellite. It weighed 184 pounds, traveled around the earth every 95 minutes, and sent back radio signals for 21 days. Today there are hundreds of earth satellites, in a variety of shapes and sizes. Some look like drums, some like balls, and some like boxes. They were sent into orbit to do many different kinds of work. Some transmit radio and television signals around the world. Some observe weather conditions. Some help ships and planes find their way. Some explore space.

Design your own satellite. Draw a picture of it or make a model. Give it a name and tell what it will do in space.

October 5

Name _____

National Storytelling Festival

It's fun to listen to a good story. At the National Storytelling Festival every year, storytellers meet to share stories and learn new ways to tell them. One evening they even meet in an old cemetery and share ghost stories!

With the class or a group of friends, tell a continuous ghost story. Everyone sits in a circle with only a flashlight for light. The tellers speak slowly and in spooky voices. One person starts the story. He or she might say, "Once upon a time I took a walk down a dark road. Suddenly . . ." The next player adds a sentence or two, perhaps, "I saw a huge black cat. Its eyes glowed with light. And right behind it . . ." Everyone around the circle has a turn. When the story gets back to the person who started it, he or she ends it, in a scary way, of course!

Remember this idea. It would be a good way to end your Halloween party.

52

October 6 Name _____

Stamp Collecting Month

One of the most popular hobbies is stamp collecting. During Stamp Collecting Month, see how many commemorative stamps you can find. Commemorative stamps are those that honor important events or people. They are easy to find and interesting to look at.

Create your own commemorative stamps. Use colored pencils or pens to make stamp designs that honor fall, your birthday, some happening at school, or another event.

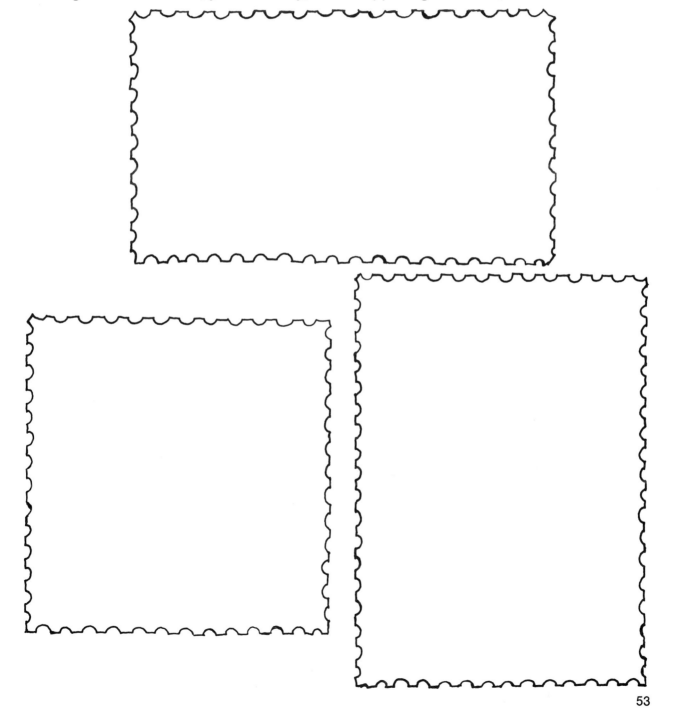

October 7

Name _____

Fire Prevention Week

During this week in 1871, two huge and disastrous fires took place. A fire that started in a barn burned much of Chicago, and a forest fire in Wisconsin burned almost all of the town of Peshtigo.

Make sure this doesn't happen in your town. Read these good ways to prevent fires. Put a check beside each rule that you follow at home.

_____ 1. Flammable liquids are used outdoors.

_____ 2. Matches are put where young children cannot get them.

_____ 3. Stoves are placed far away from walls.

_____ 4. There are no bare wires on electric cords.

_____ 5. No one in the house smokes in bed.

_____ 6. Greasy rags and oily cans are kept away from furnaces.

_____ 7. Electric appliances are not left plugged in.

_____ 8. The chimney connected to a wood stove is cleaned every month.

_____ 9. Everyone knows how to get out of the bedrooms if there is fire.

Add your own sentence about fire safety. _____

_____

_____

_____

October 8

Name _____

A World Series Record

On this day in 1956, a baseball record was made. Don Larson, a player for the New York Yankees, pitched the only perfect World Series game ever played. That meant that no batter on the Brooklyn Dodger team had a hit or a walk.

Pitch your own perfect game. Answer these questions and solve this baseball crossword puzzle.

ACROSS
 2. Come as soon _____ you can.
 4. The people who hit the ball are called _____ .
 7. The nine players on a side are called a _____ .
 8. The pitcher threw the ball _____ the batter.
10. When a batter gets home, he scores a _____ .
11. The object of the game is for the batter to _____ the ball.

DOWN
 1. Players hit the ball with a _____ .
 3. Sometimes a batter manages to _____ an extra base.
 4. Players hit a _____ .
 5. "I _____ going to make a hit," said Jane as she swung the bat.
 6. If a batter swings and misses, it is a _____ .
 9. After three strikes, a batter is _____ .

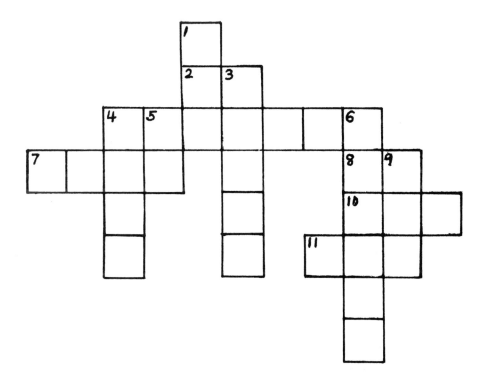

October 9

Name _____

Adopt-a-Dog Month

When Bill told his dad that October was Adopt-a-Dog Month, he agreed that Bill could adopt one. The whole family went to the dog pound to find a dog. Here are the ones they saw. Now they had to decide which one to pick.

"The St. Bernard wouldn't fit in the doghouse," said brother Jim.
"Don't get one with too long hair," pleaded Mother.
"Find one gentle enough for me to play with," begged sister Patty.
"Let's get one that doesn't bark too much," said Grandmother.
"I want one big enough to run in the park with me," said Bill.

What dog do you think the family chose? _____

October 10   Name_____

A New Cleaning Material

In 1933 the first soapless cleaning material was sold. It was called a *detergent.* Detergents help get clothes cleaner by lowering the surface tension of water. Surface tension is like a kind of skin on the water. When we lower its surface tension, water expands and spreads out and is absorbed in material more quickly so the dirt will lift out.

Get two glasses. Fill one with clear water. Fill the other with water in which you have stirred some detergent. Skim off the suds. Now sprinkle a little pepper very gently into the glass with clear water. The pepper will float on the clear water for quite a while.
   Now sprinkle the same amount of pepper very gently into the glass with the detergent. Notice how quickly the pepper gets wet and sinks to the bottom.

57

October 11

Name_____

A Great Lady

Eleanor Roosevelt was born on October 11, 1882. She was the wife of our 32nd president, and she is honored for what she did to help the young and poor around the world.

Mrs. Roosevelt's life was not always easy. Her husband became crippled with polio when their five children were quite young. He never walked again, except with braces. People who did not like her husband often criticized her. But she did what she felt was right.

She once said, "No one can make you feel inferior without your consent."
Look in the dictionary.

What does inferior mean? _____

What does consent mean? _____

Print Mrs. Roosevelt's statement on a sheet of paper. Color a design around it and take it home to hang by your bed. When you have a bad day, think about this sentence.

Remember, no one can make you feel as if you are not worth much, unless you agree with them.

October 12   Name _____

Hurrah for Columbus!

In 1492 Columbus landed at an island in the West Indies that he called El Salvador. We remember Columbus best for this first voyage, but he actually made four trips from Spain to America. He explored Cuba, Haiti, parts of Central America, and even the coast of South America. Study this time line, then answer the questions below.

Columbus born	Began first voyage	Began second voyage	Started home from second voyage	Left on third voyage	Began fourth voyage	Columbus died
1450	1492	1493	1496	1498	1502	1506

1. In what year was Columbus born? _____

2. When did he leave on his first voyage? _____

3. How long was he gone on his second voyage? _____

4. His third voyage started in _____

5. His fourth voyage began _____

years after his first one.

6. How old was Columbus when he died? _____

59

October 13

Name_____

Visit a Food Festival

Many communities have fall carnivals and festivals to honor foods they grow or make. There are food festivals to celebrate sauerkraut, gumbo, oysters, okra, chowder, apples, brussels sprouts, pumpkins, peanuts, and much more. People come from many miles to eat the food, watch contests, and enjoy special music.

Pretend you are planning a food festival for your neighborhood. Tell some of the activities you'd have (a tangerine tango?), describe the foods you'd serve (apple fritters?), and decide what contests you'd hold (potato bag race?). Make sure everything has something to do with the food you have selected.

My food festival will honor _____ .

_____
_____
_____
_____

60

October 14

Name _____

Faster Than Sound

The first person to fly faster than sound was Captain Charles Yeager. On October 14, 1947, his rocket plane, called *Glamorous Glennis*, reached a speed of 670 miles per hour and an altitude of over 7 miles.

A flight faster than sound is called *supersonic*. Look up this word in the dictionary. What does it mean?

_____

Below are listed some machines and animals that can move fast. Can you rearrange them in order of their speed? Start with the slowest one and end with the fastest.

space shuttle *Columbia*
cheetah
Glamorous Glennis
racehorse
first airplane
falcon
antelope
man
automobile
Boeing 747 jet

October 15

Name _____

White Cane Safety Day

A cane is a very useful device for a blind person. By swinging it back and forth and tapping it on the ground, he or she can avoid any holes or other obstructions. The canes are painted white so sighted persons will recognize that the user cannot see. Each year since 1964, the president has set aside October 15 as a day to recognize white canes.

Borrow a cane from an older friend or get any long stick. Put on a blindfold and try to walk slowly across the school lawn. (Make sure someone is with you so you don't walk into the street or bump into something that could hurt.) It will be very difficult to find your way at first, but after some practice you'll be able to avoid obstacles on the lawn. When you get back to your room, write two sentences to tell how you felt when you couldn't see.

October 16

Name _____

Father of the Dictionary

Today is the birthday of Noah Webster, born in 1758. He spent almost all his life working on books about words. His first one was a spelling book that schools used for over 100 years. But we remember him most as the author of the first American dictionary. After more than 25 years of work, *An American Dictionary of the English Language* was published. It consisted of two volumes and had 70,000 entries. Imagine working that long on one project!

Write the name of a dictionary in your classroom. _____
Use it to find five words that begin with the initial of your last name. Write down the words and their definitions.

_____

_____

_____

_____

_____

Write a sentence using at least two of these words.

_____

_____

October 17

Name _____

Black Poetry Day

Jupiter Hammon, born in 1711, was the first black American to publish his own poetry. On Black Poetry Day we honor Mr. Hammon and all other black poets.

Find copies of poems by black poets like Langston Hughes and Gwendolyn Brooks. Copy four lines from one of their poems that you like.

_____
_____
_____
_____

Write a poem of your own. Make it at least four lines long. Write about a friend, a pet, something in nature.

_____
_____
_____
_____

Would you like to share your poem? If you do, ask your teacher if you can read it to the class. Maybe you would rather keep it to yourself. That's O.K., too.

October 18

Name_____

A New Purchase

A purchase by the United States was once called silly and a waste of money. On October 18, 1867, we paid Russia $7,200,000, or two cents an acre, for a large piece of land that is now one of our states.

Answer these questions about some of our other states. If you do them correctly, the first letters of the answers will spell the name of this large state.

1. If the states were listed in alphabetical order, the first one would be _____ .

2. Wyoming would be the _____ one in the list.

3. The first 13 states stretched along the coast of the _____ Ocean.

4. Florida is in the _____ part of the United States.

5. The state where the Kentucky Derby race is held is _____ .

6. All of our states together are called the United States of _____ .

1.____ 2.____ 3.____ 4.____ 5.____ 6.____

What state do you live in?_____

Write a sentence telling why you like your state._____

October 19

Name_____

Fingerprints, Anyone?

Every person's fingerprints are different from every other person's. No two sets are alike. For over 80 years, people have been identified by their fingerprints.

Everyone at Watertown High School in South Dakota had dirty fingers on this day in 1936. The students listened to an FBI agent say that no one was really "lost" if his or her prints were recorded. Then the entire student body was fingerprinted.

Have you ever really looked at your fingerprints? Press one finger at a time on an ink pad and make a set of your prints.

Right Hand

Thumb	Index	Middle	Ring	Little

Left Hand

Thumb	Index	Middle	Ring	Little

Compare your prints with a friend's. Can you see why they are a good clue to identification?

October 20

Name _____

Greatest Show on Earth

When P.T. Barnum opened his circus in 1873 in New York, he called it the greatest show on earth. It featured animals, clowns, acrobats, and a midget known as General Tom Thumb.

Find one of Barnum's circus animals by solving these multiplication problems. Color gray any area whose product is 20 or more. Leave the other areas white. When you are done, you will find one of the largest animals in the circus.

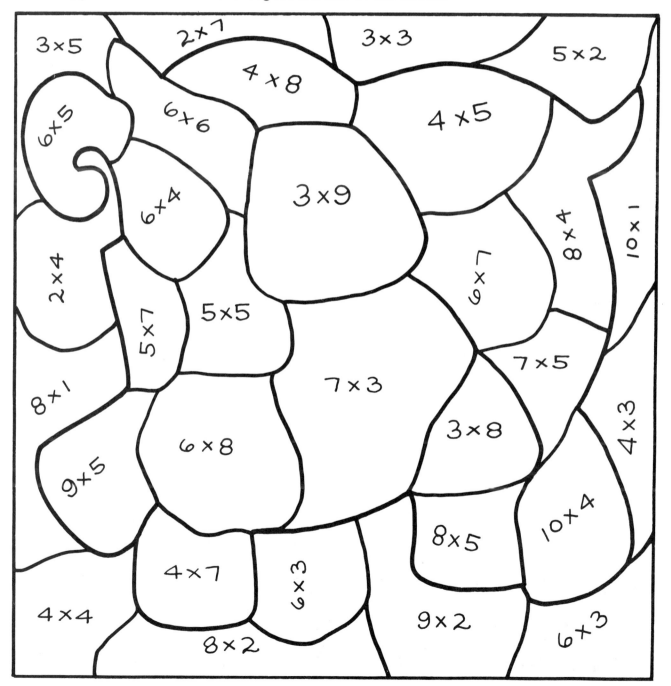

67

October 21

Name _____

First Electric Lamp That Worked

For 13 months, Thomas Edison tried to make an electric light bulb. He knew it would work if he could find something that would get hot enough to give off light but not burn. He finally found some special cotton fibers that would work. When the discovery was announced, special trains took people to Menlo Park, New Jersey, so they could see the lighted bulb in Mr. Edison's laboratory.

Today a thin tungsten wire is used instead of cotton. When it gets hot from the electricity going through it, it takes on a glow that gives us our light.

Think about the electric lights in your home.

How many bulbs are there in your kitchen? _____

In your bedroom? _____

In the living room? _____   Add them up _____

Aren't you glad Mr. Edison made his discovery?

When people called Edison a genius, he said, "Genius is one percent inspiration and 99 percent perspiration."

Write a sentence explaining what he meant.

_____

_____

October 22

National Horse Show

On this day in 1883, the first national horse show opened at Madison Square Garden in New York City. There were 187 exhibitors. This show has been held every year since. It is the largest horse show in the United States.

At a horse show, horsemen parade their horses around the arena, to show the different ways the horses can walk or run. They jump them over hurdles and show how quickly they can go through an obstacle course without touching or knocking over anything.

Enter your horse in this contest and win your own blue ribbon. You and your horse started at 3:00 and got to each place in the amount of time shown in the list of stations. Mark each station with the time you arrived there.

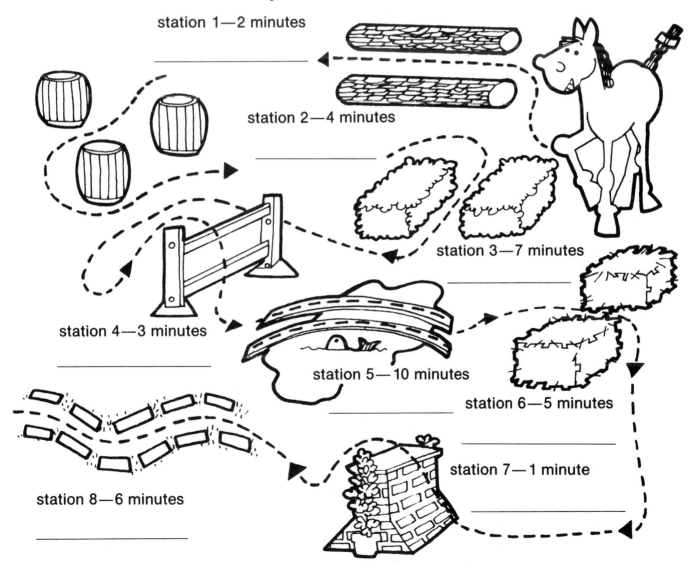

station 1—2 minutes
station 2—4 minutes
station 3—7 minutes
station 4—3 minutes
station 5—10 minutes
station 6—5 minutes
station 7—1 minute
station 8—6 minutes

October 23

Name _____

Swallows Leave

Thousands of swallows nest around the mission church in San Juan Capistrano, California. But each year on this day they begin to leave for a winter home farther south. No one knows for sure why they pick this day, but experts say that as the days get shorter, the birds realize it is time to leave. Everyone who lives nearby knows they will return on March 19, when sunlight makes the days longer.

This swallow will seem to really fly. Cut out the body and wings and color both sides of each piece. Tape wings in place. Attach a thread to the body and fasten the other end of the thread to the end of a pencil or small stick. Swing around over your head.
 If you wish, you can make a mobile by hanging several birds from a wire coat hanger.

October 24   Name _____

It's Message Time

Two important events happened on this same day in 1861. A telegraph line from the East to the West coasts was completed, and the Pony Express came to an end.

For 19 months the Pony Express had left St. Joseph, Missouri, at noon each day and arrived in Sacramento, California, about ten days later. It cost $5 to send a letter weighing a half ounce. Now, a message could be sent from New York to San Francisco. It cost $6 to send 10 words, but it would arrive in just a few minutes.

Why was the Pony Express no longer needed?

_____

_____

Write a telegram asking a cousin in San Francisco to visit you in New York for three weeks next summer. You can send 10 words for $6. More words will cost $.75 each. How much will your telegram cost? Can you do it for $6?

_____

_____

Write your cousin's answer. Be sure to say when he or she will arrive in New York. How much will this one cost?

_____

_____

October 25

Name_____

Picasso's Birthday

Pablo Picasso, born in 1881, has been called the greatest painter of the 20th century. He began to paint when he was 14 and had made over 20,000 works of art before he died when he was 91. Many of his sculptures were made from things he found. He once made a bull's head from the seat and handlebars of a wrecked bicycle!

Artists have the ability to select one small scene from all of the outdoors. You can do the same thing. Ask your teacher if you can frame an area about 9" × 12" in a window with tape. Stand three feet from the window and look through your frame. Make a drawing of what you see, the same size as your area through the window. Tape it in place on the window to show others.

October 26

Name_____

Erie Canal Opened

This important national waterway was opened in 1825. It stretched 363 miles between two New York cities, Buffalo and Albany. Now people could go from New York City to Albany on the Hudson River, travel on the canal to Buffalo, and then take a ship across the Great Lakes to settle in the Midwest. Later they would send their farm products east the same way. Boats were pulled through the canal by mules or horses walking on a path, called a *towpath*, beside the canal.

Made a 3-D canal scene. Fold a 9" × 12" sheet of construction paper in half lengthwise, and open it up so the fold faces you horizontally. Along the top half, about 3" from the top edge, sketch a light line. Color the paper blue from this line to the bottom of the paper to make the canal. Color tan a narrow strip at the top edge of the canal to show the towpath. Cut out and color two mules and a canal boat. Glue the mules to the top of the paper so their feet touch the tan strip and they seem to be walking on the towpath. Make a fold on the bottom edge of the boat and staple fold to the canal, so the boat will stand up. Make sure mules are ahead of the boat. Tape a string from the boat to the mules. Then stand the top half of the paper up, and your canal scene is ready for action!

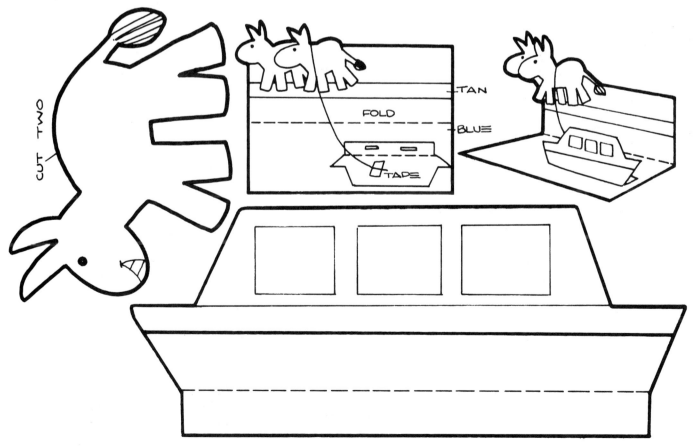

October 27

Name _____

Good Bear Day

Good Bear Day honors the memory of President Theodore Roosevelt, who was born in 1858. He was the first president to ride in an automobile, to submerge in a submarine, and to fly in an airplane. But did you know that a stuffed animal toy was named after him? During a hunting trip, he found a baby animal and saved its life. An artist drew a picture of him holding this animal. Soon toy makers everywhere were naming stuffed animals after the president's nickname.

To find the animal, draw lines to connect the letters that spell President Theodore Roosevelt. When complete, you'll find the toy named for him. Did you ever have one of them?

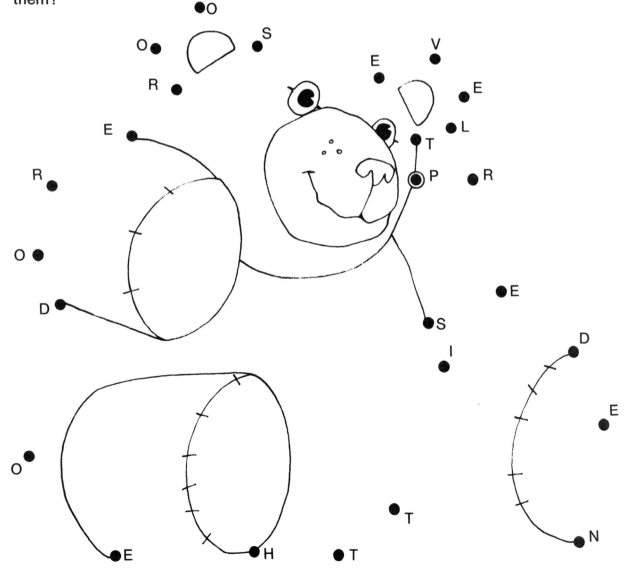

October 28   Name_____

The Lady with the Lamp

The Statue of Liberty was dedicated today in 1886. This gift from the people of France stands on an island in New York Harbor. Immigrants from Europe were sure to see it as their ship brought them to the United States. The statue gave them courage as they came to a new land.

Complete these sentences.

1. People who come from another land are called_____

2. The statue's official name is Liberty Enlightening the World. What does enlighten mean?_____

3. A poem on the statue says, "I lift my lamp beside the golden door." What was the golden door?_____

In 1986 the United States celebrates Liberty's 100th birthday. Look in newspapers and magazines for articles about the statue and the celebration.

October 29

Name _____

National Magic Week

This week honors the memory of Harry Houdini, one of America's greatest magicians. He was born on March 24, 1874, and died on Halloween, 1926.

You can become a magician, too. Try these tricks on your family and friends.

Tell people that you can hold the ends of a piece of string and tie a knot in it without letting go of the ends. When they say you can't, prove it by folding your arms, picking up the string ends, and then unfolding your arms.

Insist that you can stand on the edge of a piece of paper 12" long and that your friend can stand on the other, yet neither one of you can touch the other. Show it can happen by sliding the paper under a closed door, with you on one side of the door and your friend on the other.

If you'd like to learn more tricks, look at the magic page each month in *Boy's Life* magazine. Or ask at the library for a book of magic tricks.

October 30

Name_____

A New Kind of Pen

In 1888 John J. Loud of Massachusetts received a patent for a pen "having a spheroidal marking-point capable of revolving in all directions." In other words, he invented a ballpoint pen.

Ballpoint pens are a far cry from the pens of our forefathers. The simplest was a wood-nib pen. To make one, find a twig about the size of a pencil. With a knife, carefully pare one end to a thin point. Dip in ink and try to write your name. You'll have to keep dipping when the point gets dry.

A better pen was made by sharpening a quill, the wing feather from a large bird. If you can find a feather, cut off the end on a slant. Make sure the inside is open so it will hold a little ink. Then you won't have to dip it quite so often.

Aren't you glad Mr. Loud made his invention?

October 31

Name _____

Booray for Halloween

Wandering through a haunted house is fun to do on Halloween. See if you can get through this one. Start at the front door and try to find your way to the back door. Trace your route with a red pencil.

On another sheet of paper, create a new maze for a brother or sister to complete.

November 1

Weather, and More Weather

In 1870 the first U.S. weather observations were made. You can make a weather instrument to predict the weather. It is called a *hygrometer* and measures the relative humidity, which means the amount of moisture in the air. When a storm is on the way, the relative humidity gets higher. When fair weather is coming, it gets lower.

Collect a glass, pipe cleaner, toothpick, a long strand of a person's hair (blond is best), and glue. Wrap one end of the hair around the center of the toothpick and glue in place. Bend the pipe cleaner across the glass's top. Lower the toothpick almost to the bottom of the glass and wrap the other end of the hair around the center of the pipe cleaner and glue in place. Watch the weather. On a clear day, mark on the glass where the toothpick points. On a stormy day, mark where the toothpick points.

Now you can make a prediction. When the toothpick points to the storm area, you can predict bad weather. Do you agree with the radio forecast?

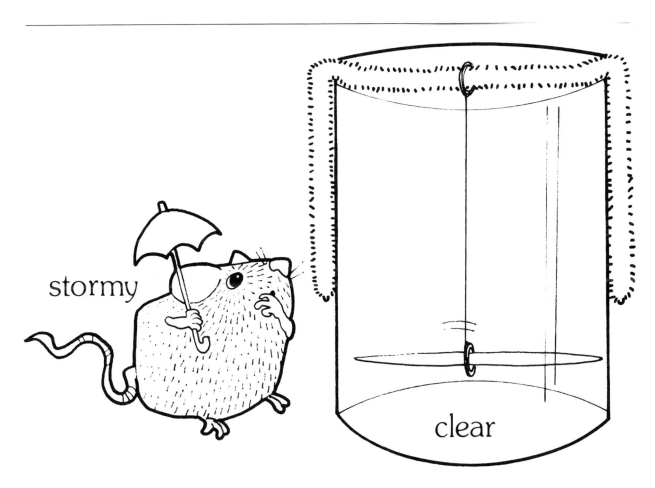

Daniel Boone

America's most famous pioneer was Daniel Boone, born in 1734. Boone and 30 men <u>blazed</u> a way from Virginia through the Cumberland <u>Gap</u> into Kentucky. It was called Wilderness Road, but it wasn't really a road, more like a <u>trail</u>. There were few bridges. In most places people crossed streams at <u>fords</u>. By 1800, 200,000 settlers had <u>migrated</u> to Kentucky over this road.

Write the underlined words in the paragraph above beside their meanings here.

_____ Persons moved from one place to settle in another.

_____ Shallow place in river where horses and wagons can cross.

_____ Cut a mark on a tree to show a route.

_____ A marked path worn by people and animals.

_____ Notch in mountains where people can move through more easily.

November 3

Name _____

Sandwich History

Thank John Montagu, born in 1718, for something you may eat for lunch today. This Englishman liked to play cards. One day he was so busy playing he didn't want to stop. A servant put meat between slices of bread for him to eat while he was playing. Mr. Montagu was a nobleman. His title was the Earl of Sandwich. And that's how the sandwich got its name.

Ask 20 people to tell you what their favorite sandwich is. List the kinds at the left. Draw a □ beside a kind of sandwich each time a person picks that kind. When done, you will have a graph showing how many of each kind were selected.

Sandwich Survey

Kind of sandwich

What kind did most people choose? _____

November 4

Name _____

Cash Register Patent

James Ritty watched a ship device for marking the propeller's movements. That gave him the idea for a machine that would record numbers and then add them up. In 1879 James and John Ritty received a patent for this machine—a cash register. To make it even more useful, there was a money drawer in the bottom. The drawer only opened when a special key was pushed. Cash registers are really special kinds of calculators. Today they can do many more things, but their most important use still is to record numbers and add them up.

Have some calculator fun. Read each story, insert the numbers one after the other on a hand-held calculator, then turn it upside down to read the answers.

1. In one week Bill's new puppy chewed 5 socks, 30 dog biscuits, 4 slippers, and 5 toy cars. When Bill scolded it, the puppy ran away and came back with Bill's

_____

2. Mark likes peanuts. On Monday he ate 80 peanuts. On Tuesday he ate 78. "Stop your eating," said his mother, "or you'll soon look like a   "

_____

3. Jim's sister runs every day. On Sunday she runs 5 blocks, on Monday 3 blocks, on Tuesday 5. On Wednesday she does not run (0 blocks), on Thursday she runs 7 blocks, on Friday 3, and on Saturday 4. Now, every time she and Jim race,

_____

Make up your own calculator quiz.

_____

_____

_____

_____

82

November 5

Name _____

Shirley Chisholm Elected

On this date in 1968, a nursery school teacher became famous. Shirley Chisholm was the first black woman to be elected to the U.S. House of Representatives. Each state elects at least one person to go to Washington, D.C., and work to pass laws that our country needs. Ms. Chisholm was elected by New York. In order to be elected, a person must be at least 25 years old. The man or woman must have been a citizen of the United States for at least seven years, and must live in the state that elects him or her.

Can you find the underlined words above in this word search puzzle? Words are across, up and down, backward and forward.

A	M	W	B	I	U	S	L	R	D	I	T	F	W	S	H
K	C	A	L	B	N	E	L	E	C	T	E	D	U	W	N
Z	J	S	G	I	S	V	A	H	R	K	S	Q	C	A	A
H	S	H	I	R	L	E	Y	C	H	I	S	H	O	L	M
O	V	I	T	C	P	N	R	A	D	O	E	R	U	Y	O
H	T	N	V	G	A	N	F	E	J	M	U	C	N	S	W
L	W	G	K	B	X	W	S	T	A	T	E	V	T	D	C
S	E	T	A	T	S	D	E	T	I	N	U	E	R	L	P
B	G	O	J	F	P	M	S	Q	U	K	D	F	Y	G	E
N	A	N	E	Z	I	T	I	C	M	D	C	O	K	E	H

November 6

Name _____

John Philip Sousa

Sing "Happy Birthday" to John Philip Sousa, born in 1854. This composer and bandmaster was called the "March King" because over 100 of the pieces he wrote were marches. Many were composed especially for the U.S. Marine Band. Mr. Sousa was its leader for over 10 years. Mr. Sousa also designed a special kind of tuba for marching bands. It is called the sousaphone, after its inventor.

Make your own instrument to have fun with. Wrap a piece of wax paper once around the teeth of a fine-tooth comb. Hold the comb loosely against your lips with the teeth of the comb up, and hum a tune through your mouth. For different effects, use different papers.

Have a class parade of comb musicians. If you can find a recording or tape of one of Mr. Sousa's marches, play it as you hum and march.

Canadian Pacific Railroad

In 1885 the people of Canada were able to travel from one end of their country to the other by train. The last piece of railroad line was completed on this day. Today Canada has thousands of miles of railroad tracks. Its trains carry passengers and all kinds of freight.

Sometimes railroads use special kinds of cars so they can carry different materials safely. Look at these cars. Draw a line from each car to the freight it might carry.

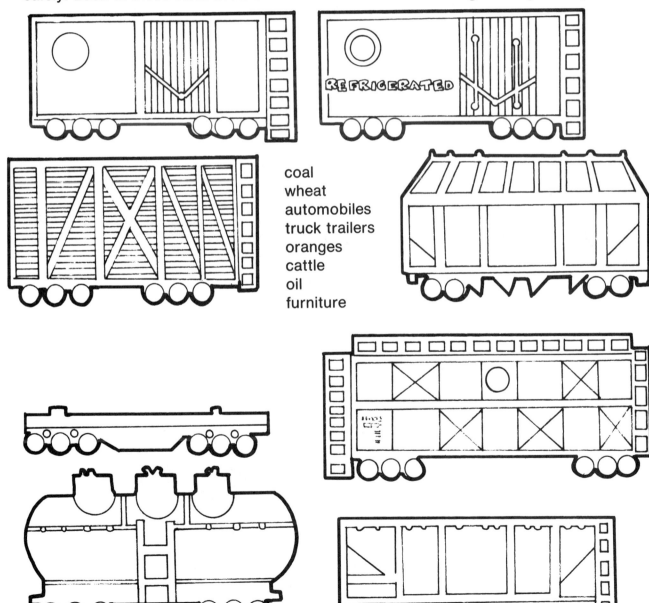

coal
wheat
automobiles
truck trailers
oranges
cattle
oil
furniture

Edmund Halley

This famous astronomer was born in 1656. When he saw a comet in 1682, he studied old records and decided this comet had already appeared many times before. He said it would come again in 1759. He was correct. Other astronomers named the comet after him.

Astronomers think a comet is like a huge dirty snowball. It is made up of frozen gases and water with dust, metals, and rocks stuck in it. As this ball moves toward the sun, the water and gases begin to evaporate. The dust and gases form a hazy cloud around the snowball and make a long tail.

Halley's Comet appears about every 75 to 78 years. The years aren't exact because sometimes the comet is seen for more than one year at a time. There are records of appearances since 240 B.C. Complete this chart below to show the years when the comet might have appeared. When will it probably come again? Get ready to watch for it!

240 B.C.	____	____	____	1607
____	____	____	____	____
____	376	____	____	1759
____	____	____	____	____
A.D. 68	____	992	1456	1910
____	____	____	____	____

November 9   Name_____

Benjamin Banneker Born

Benjamin Banneker was born in 1731. This free black person was a successful farmer, surveyor, mathematician, and astronomer. He is remembered for three very important reasons:

1. He created a clock by carving every gear and clock piece from wood. It ran for over 50 years.
2. He helped mark the boundaries of the District of Columbia and helped map the design of the city.
3. He studied the stars to get the information he needed for an almanac he wrote. The almanac contained weather predictions, times of high and low tides, and reports of the behavior of the sun and moon.

Make patterns of some of the constellations Banneker saw. Cut out these circles and make holes at the dots with a small hole punch or a round toothpick. Color circles black. Tape each circle to a flashlight, making sure all of the glass is covered. Turn out all the lights. Flash the light against a wall.

87

November 10

Triton Goes to Sea

November 10, 1959, was a big day for the submarine *Triton*. Her first duty had just been assigned—to go around the world. But she would try to make this round-the-world trip underwater. And she did! Her 13 officers and 135 crew members went 41,500 miles in 84 days without ever surfacing.

Do you know how a submarine works? It has two outside walls, called *hulls*. When a submarine wants to submerge, or go underwater, valves are opened so water can come in between the hulls and make it heavier. When it wants to surface, or come up, compressed air is blown between the hulls to force the water out and make the submarine lighter.

Make a model to show how a submarine goes up and down. You will need a mixing bowl, a small medicine bottle, a flexible straw, and water. Ask an adult to help you cut two holes in the top of the medicine bottle. Put the straw through one of the holes. Fill the bowl with water and place the bottle with its top on tight in the bowl. As water fills the bottle (through the hole without the straw in it), it will sink. Then blow through the straw to fill the bottle with air, and it will rise.

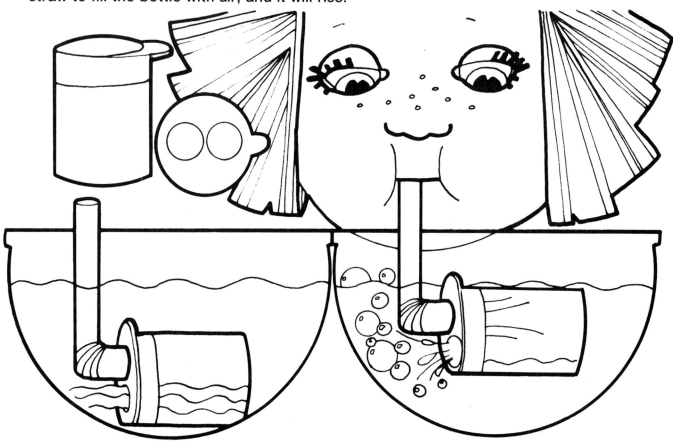

November 11

Name _____

Veterans Day/ Remembrance Day

The fighting in World War I ended on November 11, 1918. Every year since then, people have honored anyone who has fought for his or her country. The United States calls this day Veterans Day. In Canada it is called Remembrance Day.

This poem is a kind of prayer to honor veterans. Copy it in your best handwriting and give it to someone who has served in our country's armed forces.

Flags today in tribute wave
For those loyal ones who gave
Of their youth, their hopes, their might
For a cause they knew was right.

Morning bells sound their call.
Pause and say a prayer for all—
All who served valiantly
That men might be ever free.

Toll of bells, drums' slow beat—
Silence falls in every street.
In each heart swells the plea:
Keep us safe, but keep us free!

First Trapeze Act

The people of Paris gasped as Jule Leotard went back and forth on a swing high in the air. They were seeing the first trapeze act ever, in 1879. But they were also interested in the costume he was wearing. It fitted him closely so nothing would get caught in his trapeze. We can thank Jule Leotard for giving us a great circus act. And also for leotards, the clothing named after him.

Some of our clothes get their names in unusual ways. They can be named after a person or place, where they are worn, or the material they are made from. Draw lines from these pieces of clothing to their definitions.

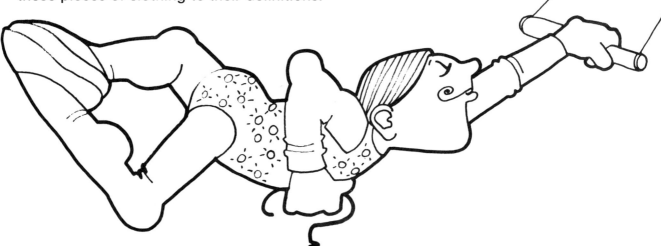

jeans	worn around the neck
leg warmers	from a French phrase, *cord du roi*, that means material of a king
tuxedo	the shape of a letter
sneakers	strong durable cotton fabric
necktie	first worn in Tuxedo, New York
T-shirt	keeps limbs from getting cold
corduroys	first made of rubber and canvas so the wearer could walk silently

November 13   Name_____

Peanut Butter Invented

In 1890 a doctor was looking for something to help sickly people become healthier. He ground up peanuts and ordered his patients to eat some of this "peanut butter" each day. Don't you wish your doctor's prescriptions were as tasty?

Peanuts and peanut butter are very nutritious. One pound of peanut butter gives you more energy than one pound of steak.

List four different ways to eat peanut butter.

_____   _____

_____   _____

What is your favorite one?_____

Birds like peanut butter, too. Make this snack to hang outside a window at school or home. You will need a pinecone, peanut butter, and birdseed. Spread the peanut butter in the open spaces in the cone. Then stick birdseed in the peanut butter. Add a string for hanging. Then watch bird friends enjoy your gift!

November 14

A Trip by Nellie Bly

Nellie Bly was a newspaper reporter. After reading the book *Around the World in 80 Days*, she decided to see if she could make the trip in less time. She left New York on this day in 1889. In France she visited Jules Verne, the author of the book that had given her the idea. He was sure a young woman, traveling alone, could not make the trip in only 80 days. But she did! She went 24,899 miles in 72 days, 6 hours, and 11 minutes.

Make two lists. In the first one, list all the ways to travel that Miss Bly could have used in 1889. Make a second list of ways you could travel today if you were going on that same trip. Some vehicles could be on both lists. To make your lists longer, read an article on transportation in an encyclopedia, or find a book in the library.

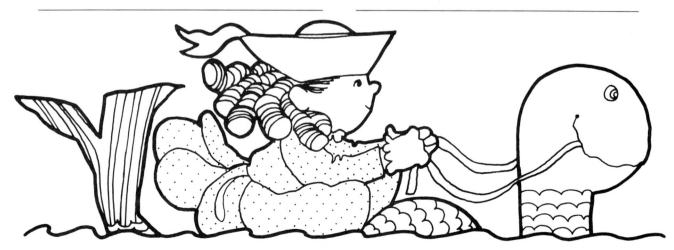

November 15　　　Name _____

National Children's Book Week

This is National Children's Book Week. It is a week to think about reading for fun and to enjoy new books. The first Book Week celebration was in 1919. Two years later, a Book Week poster was designed to encourage boys and girls to read. Its slogan was "More Books in the Home." A new poster has been designed every year since then.

Create your own Book Week poster. Use the slogan of the first poster, "More Books in the Home," and create a design or picture to go with it. Ask your teacher if you can display your poster in the school hall.

November 16 Name_____

First Family Moves to White House

In 1800 John and Abigail Adams and their family moved into the White House. But the house was far from finished. In fact, the large East Room was just a bare space. Today the White House is a beautiful home where the president lives and works. You and I can visit five of the White House rooms—the large East Room, where the president's guests are entertained; the Blue, Red, and Green rooms, where most of the furnishings are one color; and the dining room, which is large enough to serve 140 people.

Create a room that people might like to visit. Draw your own or cut pictures of parts of rooms from magazines and arrange them on a large paper. Decide on a name—Gold Room, Country Room, Seaside Retreat—that goes with the kind and color of furniture you put in it.

Do you believe in ghosts? Every so often, people think they see the ghost of Abigail Adams. She seems to float in and out of the East Room, where she used to hang laundry to dry.

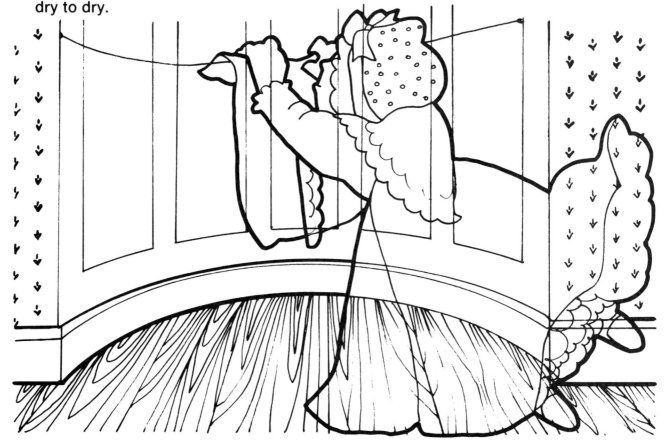

November 17

Suez Canal Opened

In 1869 ships began to move through this important canal. Canals are manmade rivers that connect two other bodies of water. They make a shortcut for ships. The Suez Canal was a real shortcut. It made the trip from England to India about 6,000 miles shorter.

Use a blue pencil to trace a ship route around Africa from England to India. Then trace a route to India by going through the canal. Today most of the ships that use the canal are carrying oil to Europe and North America. With a red pencil trace a route from the oil fields to England through the canal. Show the route they would have to follow if there were no canal.

Standard Time

During the early days of our country, every town set its own time. When the sun was directly overhead, it was 12:00 noon. At a town 50 miles east, noon had come several minutes earlier; for towns 50 miles west, it was not yet 12:00. As the railroads began to travel west, time became very confusing. Train conductors had to change watches every few minutes. People missed trains because the station was a few miles away, where the time was different.

The confusion ended at noon on November 18, 1883. The United States was divided into four time zones, with one hour difference between them.

Look at the map above, then tell what time it is in:

Des Moines _____ Toronto _____
Denver _____ Miami _____
San Francisco _____ Dallas _____
Vancouver _____ Seattle _____
Boston _____ St. Louis _____
Phoenix _____ Calgary _____

November 19

Name _____

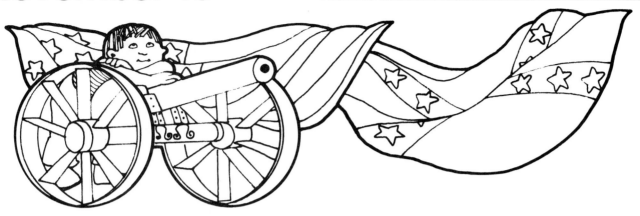

The Gettysburg Address

Thousands of people were killed on both sides in the great battle of Gettysburg during the Civil War. Part of the battlefield was set aside as a burial ground for those killed. On this day in 1863, the U.S. government dedicated this cemetery. President Lincoln was a special guest at the ceremonies but not the main speaker. His speech had only 300 words and lasted only two minutes. But the words he said will always be remembered.

Lincoln used some interesting phrases in his speech. Answer these questions about some of them. Use a dictionary if you need to.

"Four score and seven years ago"—How long ago was that? _____

What year was he referring to? _____

"that that nation might live"—How does a nation live? _____

_____

"we cannot consecrate this ground"—What does *consecrate* mean? _____

_____

"that these dead shall not have died in vain"—Explain the meaning of "in vain."

_____

"government of the people, by the people, for the people"—What sort of government is that? _____

_____

November 20

Name _____

Peregrine White Born

One day after the *Mayflower* reached New England, a baby girl was born. She was the first child born in Plymouth Colony. Her parents called her Peregrine which means "having a tendency to wander."

Why do you think the Whites gave their child that name?

_____

What is your name? _____

Were you named after a person, a place, because of a certain event or date, or just because someone liked the name?

_____

What do you think these people might be named for?

Holly _____

Patrick _____

June _____

Years ago many parents gave their children names that had special meanings. For example: Amy means *beloved*, Harold means *warrior*, John means *God's gracious gift*, Susan means *lily*, Karen means *pure*, Thomas means *twin*, and Frank means *free*. Today most people don't think about meanings, but they are fun to find out about. Look up an encyclopedia article about names, and make a list of names and their meanings. Or ask at the library for a book of names.
Can you find out what your name means?

November 21

Alaska Highway Opens

During World War II, the United States needed to be able to travel to Alaska by land. So in March 1942, army engineers began building a road. In about eight months, they finished a narrow dirt road 1,500 miles long—the Alaska Highway. They had built more than 6 miles a day through hills, mountains, swamps, forests, mud, and huge swarms of mosquitoes.

Pretend you were one of the workers on this important road. Design a bumper sticker to tell others about the road. Make it about 4" × 18". Use letters large enough to be seen far away. Here are some ideas for what your sticker might say:
   Happiness is working on the Alaska Highway
   Alaska Highway—Mosquito Trail
   The Mud Route to Alaska

November 22

SOS Signal

In 1906 an international call for help was adopted. Ships of any nation could send the letters SOS by Morse code—three dots, three dashes, three dots—and help would be on the way. The letters do not stand for anything but they are easy to send and to remember, even in an emergency.

Pretend you became lost on a mountain or in the desert. Tell how you could create an SOS pattern to let airplane searchers know where you are.

_____

_____

_____

_____

Suppose you became separated from your friends on a hike in the woods. How could you send an SOS message?

_____

_____

_____

November 23

Zibelemarit

Swiss Onion Market Day (Zibelemarit) is held on the fourth Monday of November in Bern, Switzerland. When the city burned down in 1405, farmers in the area helped to rebuild it. To thank them, the city gave farmers the right to sell their products in Bern. Each year tons of onions are piled on the city square in front of the Federal Palace. People come from miles around to see and buy farm products.

Celebrate Zibelemarit by asking a friend this riddle:
  I went to the garden and got it,
  Came to the house and cried over it.
  What was it?
Write your own riddle about this or any other vegetable.

An old weather saying goes this way:
  When an onion's skin is very thin, mild winter's coming in.
  When an onion's skin is very tough, the coming winter will be cold and rough.
When you get home today, ask your mother or father if you can look at an onion. Examine its skin. What does the onion say? Will the winter be mild or rough?

November 24

Name_____

Patent for Barbed Wire

In 1874 Joseph F. Glidden received a patent for a way to make barbed wire. He placed metal pieces (barbs) between two wires and twisted the wires to hold the barbs in place.

Farmers in the East had been building stone walls or fences made of wood. But in other parts of the country, there were no boulders and very few trees. With barbed wire, now these farmers could have fences, too.

Some of the common materials for fences and walls today are wood, concrete, wire, and even plastic. Look out of your school window. Do you see any fences or walls? Describe them, or draw pictures of them.

November 25   Name_____

Ship Sank in Harbor

In 1780 the English ship *Hussar* was on its way to New York with money and supplies. It never arrived. In the harbor, within sight of land, it sank, and with it went 900,000 gold coins. No trace of the ship or its money has ever been found. For hundreds of years hunters have looked for lost treasures and hidden money. Only a few have been successful.

This map and clues will lead you to treasure hidden in the hills of a pirate's island. Maybe you'll be lucky and locate it. On the map, 1 inch is equal to 500 yards. Remember directions and use a ruler to trace your route.

Start at the ship's wharf. Go north 250 yards, then east 500 yards, then northwest 750 yards to the stream. Cross the stream, then go north 1,000 yards to the gorge. Descend into the gorge, then walk east along bottom of gorge 250 yards. Last of all, walk 500 yards northwest. Put an X at the place where you would start digging. Happy hunting!

November 26

First Lion in the United States

In 1716 a notice in the *Boston News Letter* announced that a "Lyon, with many other rarities" would be on display. Many people rushed to see this strange animal.

Pretend you are a boy or girl living in Boston in 1716. Your father takes you to see an animal you have never heard of before. You look at it very carefully so you will always remember it. When you get home, your grandmother asks what it looks like. Write three sentences to describe the lion you saw.

November 27

Name _____

National Family Week

National Family Week is a time to think about families and the fun they can have together. A family is any group of people who live and love together. And this is the week of Thanksgiving, a time when families usually get together.

Family fun can be visiting the zoo, having a picnic, playing a game together, watching a TV movie together, reading a book out loud, and many other things. Draw a picture of a family group having fun together.

November 28

Name _____

First U.S. Car Race

This race took place in 1895. Over 80 cars were entered, but when the race began, only 6 were able to start. There were 3 foreign cars. One of the American cars had a gasoline engine. The rest were electric or steam. The course was 52 miles on a snow-covered road from Chicago to Waukegan, Illinois. The gasoline car finished first and won the $2,000 prize. The only other car to complete the race was an American electric car. It had to be pushed several miles. The winning driver was James Duryea, who drove a car invented by his brother Charles.

Can you win this race? Begin at Chicago and complete each problem along the way. If you are correct, you should arrive at Waukegan with the number 338.

Start with 84 cars.	Subtract number of cars that would not start.	Add miles the race was long.	Subtract one driver and one passenger.
			Multiply by number of cars that completed race.
Divide by number of Duryea brothers.	Subtract day of the month when race was held.	Divide by number of foreign cars in race.	Add amount of prize money.
Waukegan 338			

November 29   Name_____

Louisa May Alcott Born

Louisa May Alcott, born in 1832, had many friends who were writers. So she began to write, too. Her best-known book is *Little Women*, the story of the March family. Many of the events in the lives of this family were based on the things that happened to Louisa and her family. She used her own experiences to make her books interesting.

Think about last Halloween. Did you go to a party, march in a parade, tell ghost stories, go trick-or-treating? Remember the funny things that happened and what a good time you had. Pretend you are writing a book called *Through the Year with Judy and Jim*. Write the Halloween chapter here. Have Judy and Jim enjoy the same things you did on Halloween.

November 30   Name_____

The First Softball Game

The baseball season was over but players didn't want to quit. So, in 1887, George Hancock invented an indoor game. He used a broomstick for a bat and a boxing glove for a ball. He called his game indoor baseball. We call it softball. By 1895 the game had moved outdoors, where we play it today.

This is the scoreboard for a game between the Jets and the Rockets. The fifth inning score is missing. Here is what the batters did in that inning. Figure out the runs made and complete the scoring.

Jets	1	0	0	2		0	2	
Rockets	0	0	1	1		0	3	

Jets
Batter 1—hit single
Batter 2—hit home run
Batter 3—out
Batter 4—walked
Batter 5—out
Batter 6—hit double
Batter 7—out

Rockets
Batter 1—out
Batter 2—hit double
Batter 3—hit single
Batter 4—out
Batter 5—home run
Batter 6—out

In the last inning, the Jets got 2 runs, the Rockets 3. Fill in the blanks below to tell what might have happened to get those runs.

Jets   Rockets

Batter 1_____   Batter 1_____

Batter 2_____   Batter 2_____

Batter 3_____   Batter 3_____

Batter 4_____   Batter 4_____

Batter 5_____   Batter 5_____

What was the final score?_____   Which team won? __ _____

Chapter 2

Reproducibles for Winter

This group of winter reproducibles begins with December 1 and continues through February 29, leaving out the last week of December. Since few, if any, schools are in session from December 25 to January 1, it seemed more important to include other dates rather than these. Chapter 4 also has pages for *Hanukkah* and for *First Day of Winter* to use on the proper days.

Special months and weeks in this chapter are National Hobby Month (Jan. 2), National Soup Month (Jan. 10), Dental Health Month (Feb. 4), Black History Month (Feb. 20), New Idea Week (Feb. 9), and Brotherhood Week (Feb. 19).

December 1

Name _____

First Drive-In Service Station

"Fill 'er up!" That's probably what the drivers said as they wheeled into the first drive-in service station on December 1, 1913. The Gulf Refining Company built the station at the corner of Baum Boulevard and St. Clair Street in Pittsburgh, Pennsylvania. It was open all night and sold 30 gallons of gas the first day.

Frank McLaughlin, who managed this first station, would be amazed at all the kinds of vehicles that drive by that corner today. Help him sort them all out. Start at the star below and write down every third letter, going clockwise around the block three times. When you are done you will have three makes of U.S. cars, two kinds from other countries, and three kinds of trucks.

December 2   Name_____

Telescope Lens Poured

On December 2, 1934, in Corning, New York, liquid glass was poured into a mold to make a lens for a telescope that would photograph the stars. The mold was 200 inches across and the glass's temperature was 2,700°F. The glass was cooled slowly, only a few degrees a day, for 11 months until it reached room temperature. Then the lens was shipped to California. People ground and polished it for many years. It finally became part of the Hale telescope on February 1, 1949. It helped scientists study stars 6 sextillion miles away. That number is written with 6, plus 21 zeros.

Can you complete this chart by writing in the figures for the huge numbers below?

one hundred_____

one thousand_____

one million_____1,000,000_____

one billion_____

one trillion_____

one quadrillion_____

one quintillion_____

one sextillion_____1,000,000,000,000,000,000,000_____

one septillion_____

one octillion_____

December 3

Name _____

First Human Heart Transplant

In 1967 in Cape Town, South Africa, Dr. Christiaan Barnard performed a new kind of operation. He transplanted a heart from a person who had just died into the body of another person. The heart is a very remarkable pump that can work for years without stopping. The right side of the heart pumps blood to the lungs. The lungs take out the carbon dioxide that has collected in the blood and fill the blood with oxygen. Blood then moves to the left side of the heart, which pumps it to all parts of the body. There the blood supplies oxygen and picks up waste substances. The blood is then pumped through the kidneys, which take out waste materials. Finally the blood goes back to the right side of the heart for another trip.

Here is a simple diagram of your heart. Some of the parts have been labeled. Can you add the other names so all the parts are labeled?

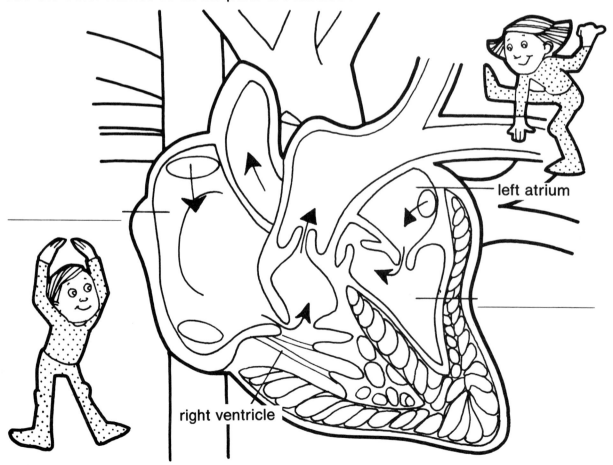

December 4   Name_____

A First, First Thanksgiving

The most famous Thanksgiving was the one the Pilgrims held. But the people at Berkeley Plantation in Virginia celebrated a day of thanks even before the Pilgrims did, on December 4, 1619. Now almost every country observes a thanksgiving. The United States celebrates in November, Canada celebrates in October.

Read this poem of thanks to yourself.

I'm thankful for the sunshine bright,
For rain and for stars at night.
I'm thankful for each flower and tree,
And all the beauty that I see.

I'm grateful for our singing birds
And for my mother's gentle words;
I'm grateful for kind friends and true;
Help me to be a good friend, too.

Cut out the poem. Draw or find a picture of some of the things it talks about. Then mount the drawing and poem on a sheet of colored paper and put it on the bulletin board.

December 5

Name _____

Jim Plunkett's Birthday

Jim Plunkett, born in 1947, was one of the best college football players ever. Once he thought about quitting college but decided not to. In his senior year in 1970, he won the Heisman trophy, as the nation's outstanding football player. He was certainly glad he had stayed in school! Mr. Plunkett's career as a professional football player is just as great as his college career was. Twice his team has won the superbowl.

You can be a football winner, too, when you unscramble these mixed-up football words.

beatrraqcuk _____

kiispng _____

adurg _____

userplwbo _____

dwoonucht _____

delif lago _____

rroadwf _____

olag tossp _____

December 6

Name_____

Mitten Tree Day

Each December the people of Baltimore, Maryland, bring pairs of mittens to hang on a mitten tree. Then, on December 6, they are sent to the Salvation Army, which distributes them.

Help the Salvation Army match up the mittens below. Draw a line from each mitten to its other half. Be careful—they are tricky! Some match because the words on them sound alike, and some because the number answers are the same. One pair matches for both reasons!

Tennis, Anyone?

Tennis was first played on this day in 1873 in Great Britain. Major Walter Wingfield got the idea from an old French game where the ball was batted with the palm of the hand. He designed the equipment, the playing area, and the rules. A year later, people began to play the game in the United States.

Play your own tennis match. First make a pair of dice. Cut out the two shapes below, fold them into cubes, and tape the sides. You can play this game by yourself or with a friend. The first person tosses the dice and adds the two numbers that come up. Put the total on the line that says first toss. If you are playing by yourself, now toss for the second player. Continue for six tosses by each player. Then add the totals for a grand score. The player with highest score is the winner.

	Player 1	Player 2
First toss	_____	_____
Second toss	_____	_____
Third toss	_____	_____
Fourth toss	_____	_____
Fifth toss	_____	_____
Sixth toss	_____	_____
Total	_____	_____

December 8

Name _____

Moving Picture with Scent

A movie with smell? In 1959 a movie about traveling in China was shown in New York City. It was called *Behind the Great Wall* and showed a tiger hunt, fishing scenes, a May Day parade, and other interesting events. Through vents in the ceiling different scents were released to make each episode more realistic.

Suppose other movies had scents. Describe the kind of smell you would expect for a movie that takes place:

at the seashore _____

in a flower garden _____

in a pizza restaurant _____

in a hay barn _____

List another place where a movie might take place. _____

Tell about the kinds of smells it might have. _____

December 9

Name_____

Christmas Seals

In 1907 Emily Bissell suggested selling Christmas seals as a way to raise money to fight tuberculosis, a lung disease. She drew the design and had the seals printed. They went on sale December 9 in Wilmington, Delaware. The city raised about $3,000.

Today many kinds of seals or stamps are made and sold to raise money. Christmas seals are still sold to raise money for lung diseases. Easter seals are sold to help crippled children. Sales of seals from the National Wildlife Federation help protect animals.

Suppose a playground was ruined by a flood. What kind of seal would you design to help raise money to rebuild the playground? Think what you might put on it—children playing; swings, seesaws, or other equipment; bulldozers leveling land. Plan your picture on scrap paper. Then draw and color it here.

December 10

Name _____

Human Rights Day

On this day in 1948, the United Nations published the Universal Declaration of Human Rights. This document lists the rights that all people should have. They are the right:

- to life, liberty, and security
- to an education
- to equality before the law
- to worship as one chooses
- to move about freely
- to associate freely with other people
- to have access to information
- to be a citizen of a country
- to work under favorable conditions and with equal pay for equal work
- to marry and raise a family

Many countries have included these rights in their constitutions.

Complete this puzzle, using the underlined words above.

December 11   Name_____

Monument to an Insect

In 1919 farmers in Alabama put up a statue to thank an insect for ruining their cotton crops. Why do you suppose they did such a thing? The insect was the boll weevil, and when it ate the farmers' cotton, they had to raise other crops. But they soon discovered that peanuts, corn, cattle, chickens, and hogs sold for much more money than cotton ever had.

Sometimes we have to do something we don't really want to and then discover it was worth doing after all. Read what happened to these boys and girls, then write what their reactions might have been.

Pete didn't want to clean the garage. But then he found a box of his Dad's old comic

books and_____

_____

Linda wanted to play tennis but her mother made her go to the shopping mall. The

sports store was having a tennis contest and Linda_____

_____

Joe and his pals were ready to play softball when his mother asked them to take some

old clothes to the community house. When they got there, they saw_____,

who had come to visit his old neighborhood, and_____

_____

Nancy was hungry for a peanut butter sandwich, but there was no bread. So she spread

it on banana slices and discovered_____

_____

December 12   Name _____

Poinsettia Day

Dr. Joel R. Poinsett was the first U.S. minister to Mexico. There he saw some interesting wildflowers. When he came home, he brought one of these plants with him. People named this beautiful plant after him and remember him on this day, the day he died in 1851.

   A Mexican legend says that a young child presented this flower at a cathedral on Christmas Eve. Perhaps that is why we have them at holiday time each year.

Make a giant poinsettia from three paper plates. Paint or crayon the fronts of the plates red, then cut them into quarters. Trim just one of the quarter pieces into the petal shape shown below. Cut a small center from yellow felt or construction paper. Stack up the quarter pieces and poke a hole through one of the outside corners. Poke a hole through the end of the petal shape also. Put a brass fastener through middle of the yellow center, through the petal, then through the quarter pieces. Bend the fastener ends back and fan out the quarter pieces to form a blossom. Use your blossom as part of your room's holiday decorations or take it home to give to someone in your family.

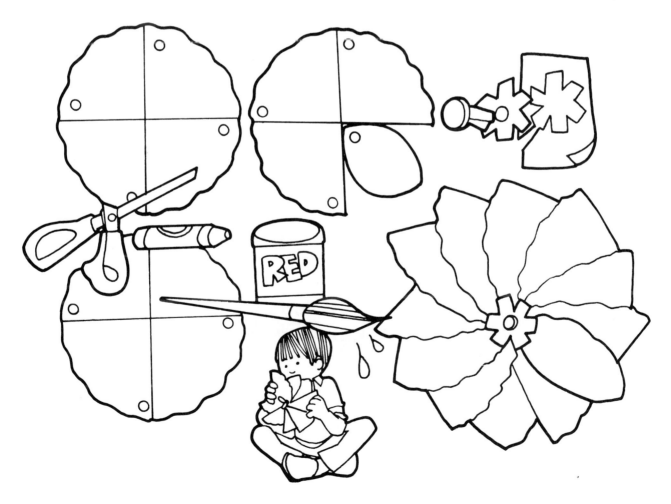

121

December 13

Name_____

Santa Lucia Day

On this day the people of Norway and Sweden celebrate Santa Lucia Day. At one time December 13 was the shortest day of the year. St. Lucia was called the queen of light, and people believed she led the way for the sun to bring longer days.

The celebration starts when the oldest girl in the family gets up early, puts on a white dress, and places a green wreath with lighted candles on her head. She serves coffee and buns to others in the family. Often hotel guests in Sweden are awakened and served coffee cakes on this day by a white-robed girl. Many communities end the day with candlelight parades.

If you are a girl, trace and cut out several candles. Cut a strip of green paper 2″ wide and about 24″ long. Measure the strip around your head and staple ends together so it fits. Paste or staple the candles around the wreath.

If you are a boy, make a star-decorated hat to wear. Get a piece of paper about 18″ square. Form it into a cone and tape the seam. Cut around the edge so it's even and it fits your head. Decorate with silver stars.

Roald Amundsen Reached South Pole

Many people had tried to reach the South Pole. Roald Amundsen and four companions finally made it by dogsled in 1911. This Norwegian explorer was also the first man to go from the Atlantic to the Pacific Ocean by sailing a ship north of Canada.

Help Amundsen reach the South Pole. Start from base camp and make your way to the South Pole by putting a number in each space. Start with a 1 (for Amundsen) and a 4 (for his companions). As you put a number in a space, add, subtract, or multiply that number with the previous number, as the operation signs indicate. Try to end up with 52, the number of dogs that left with the men.

If you have time, make your own puzzle on the other side of this sheet. Start at the South Pole with 52 and put in your own numbers and symbols so you return to base camp with 12, the number of dogs that made it back.

December 15

Name _____

Halcyon Days

For about a week before winter begins and for a week after, there is usually calm weather. Ancient people explained the reason by saying a bird (called the halcyon) had built a nest on the ocean and was keeping the winds quiet until the eggs hatched. They called this time Halcyon Days. Today we give this name to any period of peace and prosperity.

Celebrate Halcyon Days by writing a poem about winter. Think about these winter things: weather, sports and games, school vacations, holidays. Make your poem as long or short as you wish. Remember, a poem doesn't have to rhyme.

_____
_____
_____
_____
_____
_____
_____

December 16

Name_____

Posada Celebration

This Mexican celebration begins today and lasts for nine days. Each evening a group of friends, pretending they are taking Mary and Joseph's journey, knock at the doors of their friends for a place to stop. They are invited in for games and fun. One of the special games is breaking a pinata. This is a decorated pottery jar, filled with candy and small gifts, that hangs from the ceiling. Boys and girls are blindfolded, and one at a time each tries to break it with a stick. When it finally breaks, everyone scrambles for the treats.

Help Maria and Jose go to six friends' homes. Follow the arrows, and tell what directions they went to get there. The first one is done for you.

From home to Bill's _____ east, south, east _____

From Bill's to Gabriele's _____

From Gabriele's to Pedro's _____

From Pedro's to Manuel's _____

From Manuel's to Elise's _____

From Elise's to home _____

December 17

Name_____

First Airplane Flight

Orville and Wilbur Wright had worked many years on a machine that could fly. Finally, in 1903, they were ready for takeoff. When Orville flew the plane for the first time, it flew 120 feet in 12 seconds. The brothers continued to make progress on their machine, and on the fourth flight, Wilbur flew 852 feet in 59 seconds.

Try these activities to give you an idea of the length and time of these flights.
1. Look at the second hand of the school clock or your watch. Hold your breath for 12 seconds. It wasn't very long, was it?
2. Look at the clock again. Start writing numerals from 1 to 100. See how far you can get in 59 seconds.
3. Use a ruler to measure the length of your classroom. Subtract that length from 120 feet. Then subtract it again, and again. How many room lengths was the distance of the first flight?
4. Can you figure out how many classroom lengths the fourth flight was? You can do it by subtracting or by dividing. Try it.

December 18

Name_____

A New Game

A new game went on sale in December 1935. It was a board game in which players bought railroads, power companies, water works, building lots, houses, and hotels. The streets were named after streets in Atlantic City, New Jersey. If players could purchase all the railroads, all the utility companies, or all the building lots on a street, they could demand large fees from other players landing on those spaces. Parker Brothers, who published the game, called it Monopoly. For about 50 years, children and adults have been playing this popular game.

Look up the word *monopoly* in the dictionary. Write its meaning here.

_____

_____

Tell why you think this is a good name for the game.

_____

_____

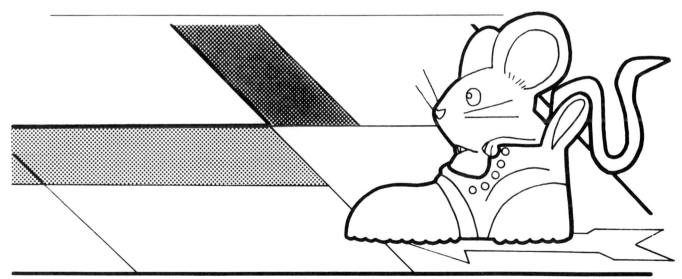

If you have a Monopoly game at home, ask if someone will play it with you tonight—after your homework is done!

December 19

First Outer Space Broadcast

Today many radio and television programs are sent to us by satellites in outer space. The first broadcast from outer space was a message from a U.S. president in 1958. President Eisenhower tape-recorded a short Christmas greeting. It was broadcast at 3:15 P.M. eastern standard time, from a rocket revolving around earth. The message was only 58 words long and ended by sending "to all mankind, America's wish for peace on earth and good will toward men everywhere."

Write a holiday greeting that you'd like to send to the people of the world. Keep it short, not more than 25 words.

_____

_____

_____

_____

_____

December 20 Name _____

Louisiana Purchase

One of the greatest real estate sales in history happened in 1803. The United States purchased the Louisiana territory from France for $15 million. This made the United States twice as big as it had been. All or part of 15 of our states were formed from this territory.

This map shows the area of the Louisiana territory and the states formed from it. Using the list below, can you label each state correctly?

Montana
New Mexico
Kansas
South Dakota
Missouri
Wyoming
Texas
Nebraska
Minnesota
Arkansas
Colorado
Oklahoma
North Dakota
Iowa
Louisiana

December 21

Name _____

Up, Up, to the Moon

In 1968 Apollo 8 left earth with three astronauts. Two days later they circled the moon and landed back on earth Christmas day. They were the first persons to see the side of the moon that we can't see from earth. Seven months later, other astronauts would make the same trip, this time landing on the moon.

When Neil Armstrong and Edwin Aldrin set foot on the moon, July 20, 1969, Aldrin described the view as "magnificent desolation." What do you think he meant?

_____

_____

_____

Start a collection of newspaper and magazine stories about travel in space. Watch for the interesting things that the astronauts in the space shuttle have been doing, such as repairing satellites and performing experiments with weightlessness.

There have been six landings on the moon. Read about them in an encyclopedia. Or ask your librarian for a book on space travel.

December 22

Name_____

Every Loaf the Same

The colonists in New England complained that sometimes the loaves of bread they bought were too small. Finally they decided to do something about it. In 1650 they passed a law saying every loaf of bread had to be the same size. Today a label on a loaf of bread usually says how much the loaf weighs. Most loaves from the large bakeries weigh one pound.

If you were buying two liters of something, what would it probably be? Draw lines to match each measurement with the food that might be bought in that amount.

two liters   hamburger

3 ounces   bread

28 grams   milk

quarter pound   cola

dozen   potatoes

one pound   eggs

gallon   spices

10 pounds   ketchup

131

December 23   Name_____

Audubon Bird Count

This is the bird-counting season. Each year since 1900, the National Audubon Society has carried out a bird census. From December 15 to January 2, more than 35,000 people in North and Central America count the kinds of birds living in their area during the winter. They try to estimate how many birds there are altogether.

Ask your teacher if you can look out the window for five minutes. Use the first chart to record how many different kinds of birds you see. Then draw a short line like this (/) on the next chart for every bird you see. Add them up to find a total.

Kinds of Birds

_____   _____

_____   _____

_____   _____

_____   _____

_____   _____

Numbers of Birds

_____   _____

132

December 24

Name _____

First Radio Program

A Christmas Eve program was the first radio program ever broadcast. It was broadcast by Professor Reginald Aubrey Fessenden in 1906 from Brant Rock, Massachusetts. There was a song, the reading of a poem, a violin solo, and a short speech. Professor Fessenden then invited listeners to report on how well they had heard him. People heard him from five miles away.

Think about a story you might read on the radio. What sound effects would you need to make it interesting? Today many of the sounds needed for a program are tape-recorded, but people used to have to make the sounds right in the studio. Here are some of the ways they made sound effects. Try them, and think up some of your own. If you have a tape recorder, tape the sounds you make and play them back for friends.

Rain—Put dried beans or peas on a cookie sheet and tilt the sheet back and forth.
Wind—Blow into the microphone, softly and far from the mike for a gentle breeze, closer and harder for stronger winds.
Galloping horse—Slap your open hands against your chest in the rhythm of a galloping horse.
Fire—Crinkle cellophane or plastic in your hand.
Jet plane—Whistle, going gradually from a very high note to a low one.
Punch—Punch your fist into the palm of your other hand.
Thud—Punch your fist into a pillow.
Engine—Turn your bike upside down and put cardboard against the spokes of a wheel as you turn it. Or turn on a blender, if you have one at home.

December 25

Name _____

Christmas

Today is the day most Christians celebrate as the day Christ was born. Over 100 countries celebrate the holiday with special church services, as well as happy get-togethers with friends and relatives.

Make this puzzle part of your celebration. Use the symbols below as clues.

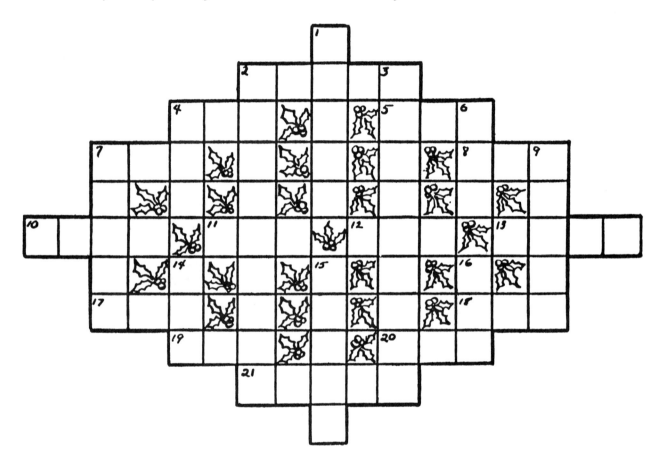

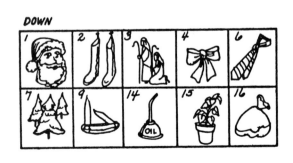

January 1

Name _____

A New Year Begins

On New Year's Day people often make resolutions. Resolutions are promises people make to do certain things during the next year. A good resolution might be to collect, before you go to bed, pencils, homework, or anything you need to take to school the next day. Put them in a special place by the door so you won't forget them in the morning.

Do you have two resolutions for this year? Write them here, then hang this paper where you will see it every day.

1. _____

_____

_____

2. _____

_____

January 2   Name_____

National Hobby Month

Do you have a hobby? Everyone should have at least one special activity that he or she likes to do in spare time. It can be playing a game or sport, collecting certain objects, making something, or practicing one of the arts like dancing or painting.

If you have a hobby, write four sentences describing it. If you don't have one, think about a hobby you might like and write four sentences telling how you plan to begin working on it. Here are some ideas for good hobbies. Collect buttons, matchbook covers, autographs, coins, stamps, postcards, or shells. Make models of cars or planes or ships. Play softball or basketball. Write poetry or stories. Learn to paint or to play a musical instrument. Whatever you choose, be sure it is an activity you really enjoy doing.

_____

_____

_____

_____

_____

_____

_____

January 3

Name _____

Earth Comes Close to the Sun

Do you like big words? Here are two you can learn and use that very few people will know.

A *perihelion* is the point where earth (or any planet) is nearest to the sun. It comes from two Greek words. *Peri* means "around or near." *Helion* comes from *helios*, meaning "sun." Today at about 5:00 P.M. eastern standard time, earth will reach its perihelion, or point nearest the sun. It will be 91,400,000 miles from the sun.

The second word is *aphelion*. If *apo* means "away from," what do you think aphelion might mean? This phenomenon will occur on July 3, at about 2:00 A.M. eastern standard time. At that time earth will be 94,510,000 miles from the sun.

Here is a diagram of the sun and some of its planets' orbits. Mark the perihelion of each planet with an X. Mark each aphelion with an O.

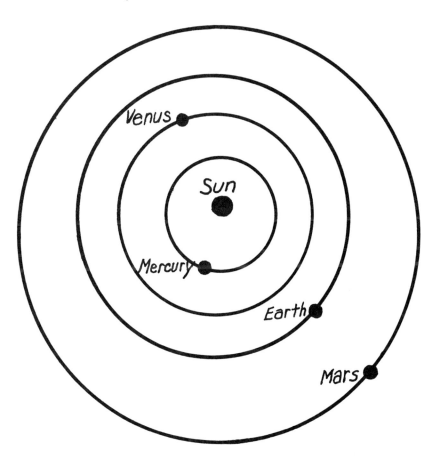

January 4

Name _____

Louis Braille Born

Louis Braille was born near Paris in 1809. He became blind from an accident when he was 3 years old. When he was 15, Braille created a system using six raised dots to stand for the alphabet, numbers, simple words, and several speech sounds. With this system, blind persons could pass the tips of their fingers over the raised dots and read. It was called braille, after its inventor.

Here is the alphabet in braille. Refer to it to translate the sentence below into braille.

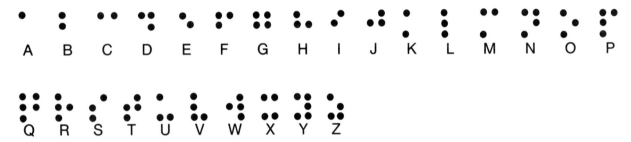

Today is the birthday of Louis Braille.

January 5 Name _____

Honor George Washington Carver

No one knows for sure just when George Washington Carver was born, so we remember him on the day of his death in 1943. This black American became famous for his research in agriculture. Carver made more than 300 products from peanuts and created over 100 different ways to eat them. He developed more than 115 products from sweet potatoes and 75 products from pecans. Because of his work, farmers in the South were able to raise and sell these crops.

Create a poster collage that will tell others about Carver. Include magazine pictures of foods made from peanuts, pecans, and sweet potatoes. Draw some scientific equipment, such as a microscope or a beaker. Show fields of plants growing. What other pictures can you think of that would relate to Carver and his work?

January 6 Name _____

Falling into a Plane?

Want to hear an incredible but true story? In 1918, during World War I, American Captain J. H. Hedly was a passenger in a Canadian plane. The pilot of the plane was trying to dodge German gunfire, so he made the plane go into a steep dive. The force pulled Hedley out of his seat and out of the plane. But when the pilot leveled off, Hedley landed on the plane's tail. From the tail he managed to climb back inside and into his seat. The plane touched down with everyone on board safe!

Put on your thinking cap and create your own incredible story—it doesn't need to be true! Make yourself the hero or heroine.

_____
_____
_____
_____
_____
_____
_____
_____
_____

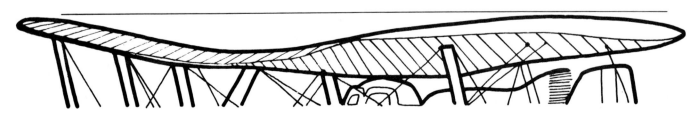

January 7

Name_____

First Harlem Globetrotters Game

In 1927 a dance hall owner hired several black basketball players to play a game twice a week in his ballroom. After a while this team traveled around the country to play exhibition games, and they became so good no one would play against them. Players began to add such funny routines as hiding the ball under their jerseys or dribbling it into the stands. Before long the comedy was the most important part of the game. Today the Harlem Globetrotters amuse people all over the world. But they are still excellent basketball players. In fact, they can only do such funny things because they are so good.

Look at this basketball picture. Can you find six things wrong with it? On another sheet of paper write the things that don't belong in the picture and tell what sport they do belong with.

141

January 8

Name _____

A Rock Star Is Born

Elvis Presley, born in 1935, was the most popular American singer in the history of rock music. Many other rock singers have followed his style of singing. Some of his popular songs were "All Shook Up," "Hound Dog," and "Love Me Tender."

Ask 20 people, both children and adults, if they know any of Elvis's songs. If so, have them tell you their favorite one. Use this chart to record your findings.

Yes	No	Favorite Song

January 9   Name _____

U.S. Balloon Flight

Jean Pierre Blanchard, from France, was the first person to make a balloon flight in America. In 1793, with President Washington watching, his gas-filled balloon lifted about a mile up into the air and traveled about 15 miles in 46 minutes. The gas in a gas-filled balloon is lighter than air. It rises the way a toy balloon that's filled with helium does.

Today many people own balloons as a hobby. Most of these are hot-air balloons. When the air in a hot-air balloon is heated, it expands and gets lighter than the surrounding air to lift the balloon.

Find a small toy balloon. Blow it up and then let the air out, so it is stretched a little. Fit the opening of the balloon over the neck of an empty soda bottle. Place the bottle in very hot water. Notice how the balloon inflates. Now put the bottle in a pail of crushed ice or very cold water. What happens to the balloon?

_____

When a hot air balloonist wants to go up in a balloon, what does he or she do? How does a balloonist make the balloon come down?

_____

143

January 10

Name_____

National Soup Month

The winter days of January are a fine time to think about how good soup tastes and how good it is for us.

Celebrate National Soup Month by performing a play with your classmates about stone soup. Do you know the story? It is about a traveler who comes to a village. He is hungry and has no money, but he does have an imagination. He convinces the villagers that he has a magic stone that will make delicious soup when he drops it in a kettle of boiling water. The villagers bring a kettle with water. He drops in the stone, stirs it, then tastes it. Each time he tastes it he says that it is coming along fine but would be better if just one thing were added. Someone always adds that thing to the pot. Eventually the soup has meat, potatoes, carrots, turnips, salt, and so on until it is a real kettle of good soup. Finally everyone eats and marvels at the magic soup. The traveler takes his stone and leaves, with the villagers never realizing they have been fooled.

    Decide who will play each part. Talk about what kind of conversations there should be between the traveler and the villagers and among the villagers. For props, get a small stone, draw large pictures to represent the ingredients and use a wastebasket for the kettle. Now on with the show!

January 11

Birthday of John A. MacDonald

Today is the birthday of John A. MacDonald. Born in Scotland in 1815, his family came to North America when he was five. At that time the northern half of this continent was called British North America. It had five provinces in the East and a colony on the West Coast. The land in between belonged to the Hudson's Bay Company. MacDonald worked to band the entire area together in a confederation. In 1867 the Dominion of Canada was formed, and MacDonald became its first prime minister.

Today Canada has ten provinces and two territories. Their names are given below. Use eight of the names to complete this puzzle.

Nova Scotia
Newfoundland
Prince Edward Island
Quebec
New Brunswick
Ontario
Manitoba
Saskatchewan
Alberta
British Columbia
Yukon (territory)
Northwest (territories)

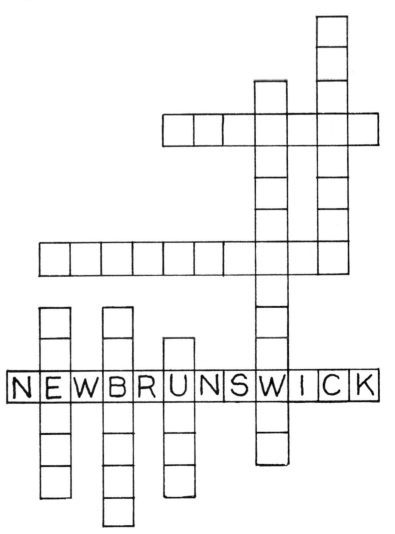

January 12

Name _____

Birthday of Charles Perrault

Charles Perrault, born in 1628, was a French writer who wrote many history books. But we know him best for a book of fairy tales. In 1697 he wrote down eight stories that people in France had been telling for many years. He put them in a book he called *Tales of Mother Goose*. Thanks to Mr. Perrault, we can enjoy "Sleeping Beauty," "Little Red Riding Hood," "Cinderella," and "Puss in Boots," among other stories.

Select one of the stories above and retell it as if you were the hero or heroine. If you have forgotten the story, ask for it in the library. Tell it to a younger brother, sister, or neighbor at home tonight.

_____

_____

_____

_____

_____

_____

_____

_____

_____

January 13   Name_____

Sarah Caldwell Conducts

From the time it opened in 1883, only men had conducted the orchestra at the Metropolitan Opera House in New York City. But, in 1976, Sarah Caldwell broke that tradition. This fine orchestra director became the first woman to conduct the Metropolitan Opera Company Orchestra.

Use your classroom dictionary to find these definitions.

Orchestra _____

_____

Conductor _____

_____

Opera _____

_____

Opera House_____

_____

Do you or does someone in your family play a musical instrument?_____

_____

Write two sentences explaining how musical sounds are made on this instrument.____

_____

Ask your teacher if she can find a record or tape of some of the music of *Porgy and Bess*. This American opera has many songs you will enjoy listening to.

January 14

Name _____

The First Moving Assembly Line

Henry Ford was not the first automobile manufacturer to use an assembly line. He was the first person, however, in 1914, to use a moving belt to put cars together. As the belt moved past the workers, each worker added a car part to the frame of the car. This system was so good that the time it took to put together a Model-T went from 12½ hours to 1½ hours. Ford was able to lower the price of his car from $850 in 1908 to less than $400 in 1916.

Assemble your own automobile. Cut out the parts and paste them on a sheet of paper. Follow the sketches to see in which order they go together. These are the steps followed in putting most cars together today.

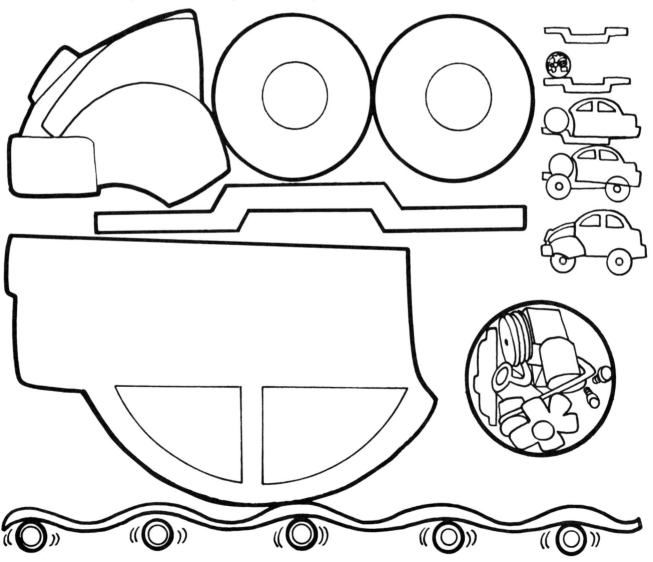

January 15 Name _____

Birthday of Martin Luther King, Jr.

Martin Luther King, Jr., born in 1929, worked to bring about equal treatment for the black people of the United States. He urged people to fight for equality in a peaceful, nonviolent way. In 1963 he led 200,000 people in a march from the Washington Monument to the Lincoln Memorial in Washington, D.C. His speech to these people described his dreams for racial equality.

Write words or phrases about King and his beliefs. Begin each one with a letter of his name. A few are started for you.

M an of _____

A lways _____

R eady to _____

T _____

I _____

N _____

L _____

U nwilling to _____

T _____

H _____

E _____

R _____

K ind and _____

I _____

N _____

G _____

J _____

R _____

January 16

Name _____

National Nothing Day

This day was first observed in 1973, "to provide Americans with one national day when they can just sit without celebrating, observing, or honoring anything." So this page is just to hold and look at. You don't have to do anything, not even read these "Knock, knock" jokes if you don't want to.

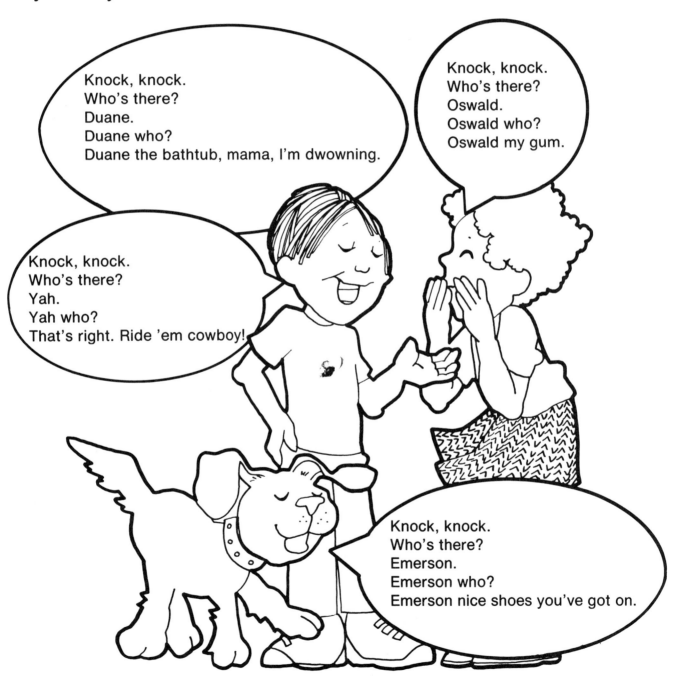

Knock, knock.
Who's there?
Duane.
Duane who?
Duane the bathtub, mama, I'm dwowning.

Knock, knock.
Who's there?
Oswald.
Oswald who?
Oswald my gum.

Knock, knock.
Who's there?
Yah.
Yah who?
That's right. Ride 'em cowboy!

Knock, knock.
Who's there?
Emerson.
Emerson who?
Emerson nice shoes you've got on.

But Nothing Day doesn't apply to school work!

January 17

Name_____

Hurray for Ben

Benjamin Franklin was born in 1706. He has been called one of America's greatest citizens. It's hard to believe that this one man accomplished all these things:

    He organized a postal system, library, hospital, newspaper, academy, fire department, police department, and antislavery society.

    He invented the Franklin stove, lightning rod, rocking chair, harmonica, and bifocal glasses.

    He discovered electricity and studied the behavior of the Gulf Stream in the Atlantic Ocean.

    He wrote an almanac and included many sayings that we still remember today.

    He worked to help establish the United States as a country and was the only person to sign four documents that were very important to this young nation.

Remember Franklin today by filling in the missing letters in the words below. Each word was mentioned in one of the sentences above.

If you would like to read a fun book about Franklin, try to find *Ben and Me* by Robert Lawson. It is a story told by Amos, a mouse who lived in Franklin's fur cap.

_ i f _ _ _ _ _ l a s s _ _

_ _ _ _ _ p a _ _ _ _

_ _ _ p i t _ _

r o c k _ _ _ _ _ a i r

_ _ i t _ _ _ t a t _ _

_ _ m a n _ _

h a r m _ _ _ _ _ _

p o s t _ _ _ _ s t e m

January 18

Name _____

A. A. Milne

Alan Alexander Milne, born in 1882, wrote many stories and poems for boys and girls. The main characters are his son, Christopher Robin, and his son's stuffed animals who come to life. Christopher Robin, Winnie-the-Pooh, Piglet, Eeyore, Tigger, and other friends have many adventures in a forest called Hundred Acre Wood. Look for Mr. Milne's books in the library.

Make a stick puppet of Winnie-the-Pooh. Trace and cut his shape from cardboard, color in his features and clothing, and staple or glue him to a narrow wooden stick. Turn a small table over on its side, kneel behind it, and have Winnie perform for the rest of the class. Maybe you and your friends can make stick puppets for several characters and dramatize one of the incidents from the Winnie-the-Pooh books.

If you can't find a picture of Winnie in a book, look for him in the children's clothing section of a Sears catalog.

January 19   Name _____

Hurray for the Tin Can!

Ezra Daggett and his nephew received a patent in 1825 to "preserve animal substances in tin." They had a small factory where they canned salmon, oysters, and lobsters. Today almost everything we eat can be bought in some form in a can.

List things you can buy that are in a can. Can you think of something for every letter of the alphabet? If you can get 20, you're a tin-can expert!

a _____   n _____

b _____   o _____

c _____   p _____

d _____   q _____

e _____   r _____

f _____   s _____

g _____   t _____

h _____   u _____

i _____   v _____

j _____   w _____

k _____   x _____

l _____   y _____

m _____   z _____

January 20

Name _____

First Basketball Game

James Naismuth, a physical education teacher, was asked to create a team game people could play inside in winter. So Naismuth thought of a kind of game that used a ball, and wrote 13 rules for playing it. He asked the school janitor to nail up two boxes to use as goals, but the janitor could only find half-bushel baskets, which he nailed in place. Mr. Naismuth's class used a soccer ball to play the first game, in 1892. Only one basket was scored, but everyone agreed it was a great game. At first, every time someone made a basket, a ladder had to be used to get the ball back! A year or so later, a net bag attached to a metal ring was used, but it was 20 years before bottomless nets were adopted.

Pretend someone has asked you how to play your favorite game. Pick any game you like and write the rules for playing it. Tell how many can play, what equipment is needed, what the playing area is like, how scores are made, and so on. Be careful. It is not as easy as you think!

January 21

Name_____

Two Great Nicknames

Two great Americans were born on this day. John Charles Fremont, born in 1813, was a great surveyor. He led several expeditions to explore the land between the Rocky Mountains and the Pacific Ocean. He is often called the Pathfinder. Can you think why?

Thomas Jonathan Jackson, born in 1824, was one of the most famous Confederate generals in the Civil War. Once, another general told his troops to stand as firm as Jackson was standing. He said, "There is Jackson, standing there like a stone wall." From then on, he was called Stonewall Jackson.

Those two men are best known by their nicknames. A nickname might describe a person's size, beliefs, things he or she likes, something he or she did, or maybe just be a shorter version of a long name.

What nickname would you give to someone who:

1. is very tall _____

2. is very small _____

3. says his favorite food is pizza _____

4. likes to invent things _____

5. is named Hildegarde _____

6. saved a kitten from drowning _____

7. is the fastest runner in the class _____

8. thinks that she will live on the moon some day _____

January 22

Name _____

First Postal Route

Before 1673 most news between the colonies was spread by peddlers or ship captains as they went from town to town or harbor city to harbor city. So it was an important day when the Boston Post Road was completed from New York City to Boston. The governor of New York announced that there would now be monthly postal service between the two cities. A government stagecoach made the first trip on January 22, 1673.

Draw the route of the Boston Post Road on this map. It went from New York City through Bridgeport, New Haven, and New London, Connecticut; Providence, Rhode Island; and into Boston.

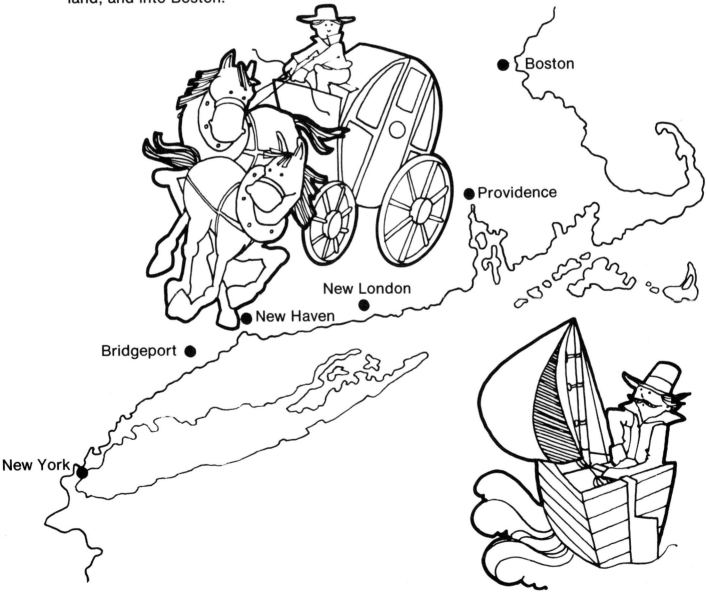

January 23 Name _____

Birth of John Hancock

Born in 1737, John Hancock was an important person in the American colonies at the time of the revolution. When the Declaration of Independence was written, he was the first person to sign it. He wrote his name in very large letters so that King George would be able to read it without his glasses. Today when a person signs important papers, we say that person has written his or her John Hancock.

This is the style of writing used in Hancock's day. Trace the letters to write your own John Hancock. Then write your name again in this style without tracing the letters.

A B C D E F G
H I J K L M
N O P Q R S T
U V W X Y Z
a b c d e f g h i j
k l m n o p q r
s t u v w x y z

January 24

Name_____

Patent for Eskimo Pie

Here's an invention you probably will want to thank its inventor, Christian K. Nelson of Onawa, Iowa, for. In 1922 he received patent No. 1,404,539 for "an ice cream confection . . . frozen . . . and encased in a chocolate covering"—in other words, the Eskimo Pie.

A patent is a government document that gives an inventor the complete rights to his or her invention. No one else can use it without permission for several years. Patents are given for inventing new things and making improvements in older ones. The first U.S. patent was given in 1790, but the first 9,957 patents were not numbered. The system of numbering patents began on July 13, 1836, when the official Patent No. 1 was issued. Most manufactured items now have their patent numbers stamped on them.

Look for the patent numbers on a pencil sharpener, stapler, filmstrip projector, or something else in your classroom. Select one item and write down all the patent numbers you can find on it.

Item Name _____

_____ _____ _____

_____ _____ _____

_____

Did you find the words *patent applied for* or *patent pending*? They mean the inventor's patent is still being considered. The United States gets over 100,000 applications a year for patents, so it takes about two years to get one approved.

January 25   Name _____

If Not the Eagle, What?

When the United States chose the American bald eagle as its national symbol, not everyone was happy. On this day in 1784, Benjamin Franklin gave his views. He said, "I wish the bald eagle had not been chosen as the representative of our country; he is a bird of bad moral character . . . generally poor and often very lousy. The turkey is a much more respectable bird, and . . . a true original native of America." He also thought the rattlesnake would be a good choice. This snake is a true North American creature, peaceful and calm when left alone. But when stepped on, it is a deadly fighter. It warns enemies of an attack, never surrenders, and rarely loses a fight.

What creature would you recommend as a national symbol? Give four reasons for your choice.

My choice is: _____

1. _____

2. _____

3. _____

4. _____

January 26

Name _____

Australia Day

For many years England punished prisoners by sending them to the American colonies. When the colonies became independent, England had to find a new place to send prisoners. On this day in 1788, Captain Arthur Phillip, with 11 ships of prison convicts, landed in this new place—Australia. This was the first English settlement there. The native people living there spoke their own language. Now all Australians speak English, but some of the original native words are still part of their language.

Here is part of a folk song. Can you understand it? Read the definitions below the song, then rewrite the song on another sheet of paper and use new words for the underlined ones. Now can you follow the song's story?

Once a jolly swagman camped by a billabong,
Under the shade of a coolibah tree,
And he sang as he watched and waited till his billy boiled,
"You'll come a-waltzing, Matilda, with me."
Down came a jumbuck to drink at the billabong,
Up jumped the swagman, "Aha," said he,
And he sang as he tucked that jumbuck in his tuckerbag,
"You'll come a-waltzing, Matilda, with me."

swagman—hobo or tramp
billabong—a channel or branch of a river
billy—can for boiling water outdoors
jumbuck—lamb
tuckerbag—a kind of knapsack for carrying food

January 27

National Geographic Society

The world's largest scientific and educational society was formed today in 1888. Its purpose is to gather and spread geographical information to everyone in the world. The National Geographic Society has helped people discover and explore unknown places and things. It has helped pay for an expedition to the top of Mt. Everest, the construction of an underwater living module, and trips to the North and South poles. Two monthly magazines, *The National Geographic* and *National Geographic World*, are read by many thousands of persons each month. The society also produces TV specials, books, filmstrips, and films.

Compose a letter to a TV station. Ask if any National Geographic special will be shown soon. Give two reasons why you think the station should present such a special. Ask your teacher to send your letter to the public broadcasting station closest to you.

January 28

First Ski Tow

The skiers at Woodstock, Vermont, were happy in 1934. Now they could be pulled up a hill instead of having to climb it. Robert Royce bought about 900 yards of manila rope and spliced the ends together to make a loop. He fit the loop over pulleys and around a wheel that was attached to a tractor. Skiers hung on to the rope, and as it moved it pulled them up the hill.

Make a model of Mr. Royce's ski tow. You will need a toy car or tractor, string, an empty spool, a pencil or piece of stiff wire, a block of wood, an empty carton or box, and tape.

Tape the car or tractor to the block of wood so the wheels don't touch the desk and will go around. Cut out the top and one side of the box or carton and make notches at the top of two sides of the box. Put pencil or wire through the spool and fit this on top of the box, in the notches. Make a loop of string and put it around the spool and the wheel. Turn the wheel to move the string. You may need to experiment to get the string tight enough.

January 29   Name_____

Baseball Hall of Fame

On January 29, 1936, baseball's Hall of Fame came into being. Five retired baseball players were chosen as the first members. They were Ty Cobb, Babe Ruth, John Peter Wagner, Christy Mathewson, and Walter Johnson. Each year since then, a committee has elected former baseball heroes for this honor. About 200 people have been elected to this group so far.

Here are 15 Hall of Famers. Write their names in the correct alphabetical order on the lines below.

Mickey Mantle   _____

Carl Hubbell   _____

Fred Clarke   _____

Martin Dihigo   _____

Babe Ruth   _____

Walter Johnson   _____

Yogi Berra   _____

Ted Williams   _____

Cal Hubbard   _____

John Peter Wagner   _____

John Clarkson   _____

Christy Mathewson   _____

Joe DiMaggio   _____

Rudy Johnson   _____

Ty Cobb   _____

January 30 Name _____

Gelett Burgess, Nonsense Expert

Mr. Burgess, born in 1866, may be one of your favorite authors, even though you have probably never heard of him. He gave us such great words as "blurb" and "goop," the poem "The Purple Cow," and many other nonsense words and verses. One book of goop tales, for example, has verses about 52 children, two for each alphabet letter. Each child's name describes a fault he or she had. Abednego didn't want to go to bed. Inkfinga had dirty hands. Nevershair would not share things. Teeza picked on others.

What do you think was the fault of these boys and girls?

Askalotte _____

Xcitabelle _____

Badinskool _____

Fibius _____

Write your own names for children with these faults.

She would not brush her teeth. _____

He liked to sing too loud. _____

He pinched his baby sister. _____

She ate with her fingers. _____

Two books, *The Burgess Nonsense Book* and *The Purple Cow and Other Nonsense*, are collections of Mr. Burgess' writings. If your library does not have them, ask your teacher or the librarian to borrow one for you and the others in your class to read.

January 31

Name _____

Explorer I Launched

In 1958 Explorer I, the first U.S. satellite, was sent into orbit. It was 80 inches long and weighed a little over 30 pounds. It discovered a magnetic belt around the earth.

The names given to rockets, satellites, manned capsules, and other space equipment are carefully chosen. Use a dictionary to look up words you don't know so you can complete these sentences.

1. Echo is a good name for a communication satellite because _____

2. A navigation satellite was called Transit because _____

3. Gemini was the name of a space capsule that carried _____ people.

4. Some of the launch rocket names are Titan, Atlas, Jupiter, and Juno. They are named after ancient _____ and _____ gods.

5. Is Nimbus a good name for a weather satellite? _____ Why? _____

6. What do you think was the purpose of Explorer I as it circled earth? _____

February 1

Name _____

Robinson Crusoe Day

On this day in 1709, Alexander Selkirk was rescued after nearly five years alone on an island. This Scottish sailor had been left at the island after he had a quarrel with his ship captain. His adventures led Daniel Defoe to write the book *Robinson Crusoe*.

Suppose you were going to be alone on an island for one year, and could only take five things. List the five things you'd take and tell why.

1. _____ : _____
_____

2. _____ : _____
_____

3. _____ : _____
_____

4. _____ : _____
_____

5. _____ : _____
_____

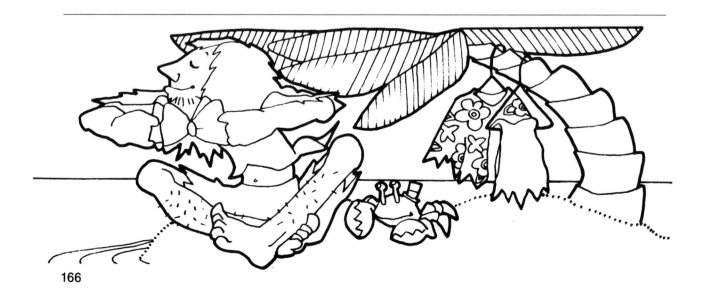

February 2

Name _____

Ground Hog Day

Today is Ground Hog Day. It came into being in a very roundabout way. See if you can follow the steps.

1. February 2 is Candlemas Day, a Catholic feast day. There is an old saying that if the sun shines on Candlemas Day, there will be six more weeks of winter.
2. A European animal called a hedgehog is supposed to wake up from its winter sleep on Candlemas Day, so the hedgehog became associated with the old saying.
3. Many early settlers to North America were from England and Germany. They found no hedgehogs here, but since the ground hog looked somewhat like it, they transferred the hedgehog's tradition to the ground hog.
4. And so today we say that if the ground hog wakes up and sees its shadow, there will be six more weeks of winter.

Do you know what a ground hog looks like? Follow this roundabout trail by connecting the numbers from 1 to 80. When you are done, you will have a picture of our friend the ground hog.

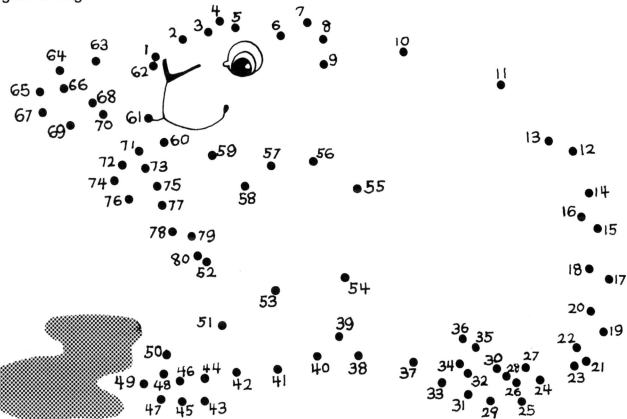

167

February 3

Name _____

Elizabeth Blackwell

Born in 1821, Elizabeth Blackwell became the first woman physician in the United States. This was an important achievement, since most medical schools would not accept women then. A few years later she started a hospital with an all-woman staff.

Dr. Blackwell would be pleased today to see how many women are working where once there were only men. Rearrange the letters below to show jobs that many women now have.

noltepehe lenniam _____ _____

otua haccimen _____ _____

relewd _____

dittens _____

ujedg _____

rooverng _____

keanrb _____

sub virred _____ _____

168

February 4   Name_____

Birthday of Lindbergh

Charles A. Lindbergh, born in 1902, made aviation history. In 1927 he was the first person to fly alone, nonstop across the Atlantic Ocean, from New York to Paris, France. He made the 3,600-mile trip in 33½ hours to win a $25,000 prize. With no radio or navigation instruments, it was a truly remarkable flight.

Pretend you are a friendly fly who accompanied Lindbergh on his flight. Tell what you did to help keep him awake for the entire trip.

_____

_____

_____

_____

_____

_____

_____

_____

February 5

Name_____

Dental Health Month

This is the month to think about our teeth and what we can do to keep them healthy. The best thing, of course, is to clean them well each day. Eating the proper foods makes a big difference, too.

Make a collage to show foods that help keep teeth strong. Include such things as raw fruits and vegetables, milk, fruit juices, fish, and chicken. Draw pictures or cut pictures from magazines.

If you like, make another collage of foods that are bad for teeth. What would they be?

February 6

Golf on the Moon

On this day in 1971, astronaut Alan Shepard hit three golf balls on the moon. They went much farther than they would have gone on earth. That's because the gravity on the moon is 6 times weaker than it is on earth. If you weighed 80 pounds on earth, you would weigh 6 times less (80 divided by 6), or $13\frac{1}{3}$ pounds, on the moon. If you could jump 2 feet into the air on earth, the distance would be 2 × 6, or 12 feet, on the moon.

Multiply or divide to turn your earth statistics into moon statistics.

	Earth	Moon
Your weight	_____	_____
Weight of a friend	_____	_____
Weight of an adult friend	_____	_____
Height you can jump	_____	_____
Length of bean-bag throw	_____	_____
Length of baseball throw	_____	_____
Choose your own statistic	_____	_____

February 7

Name _____

The Beatles in the United States

There was great excitement in New York City in 1964. This was the day the rock group called the Beatles arrived from England to appear in the United States. The Beatles were the most popular group in the history of rock music. More of their records have been sold than any other popular-music records in history. The names of the members—John Lennon, Paul McCartney, George Harrison, and Ringo Starr—are known throughout the world.

The word *Beatles* has a long ē sound. Look at the words in this puzzle. Color red every section that has a word with a long ē sound. Color blue every section that has a word with a long ī sound. Color the other sections yellow. If you do them correctly, you will find some of the instruments played by the Beatles.

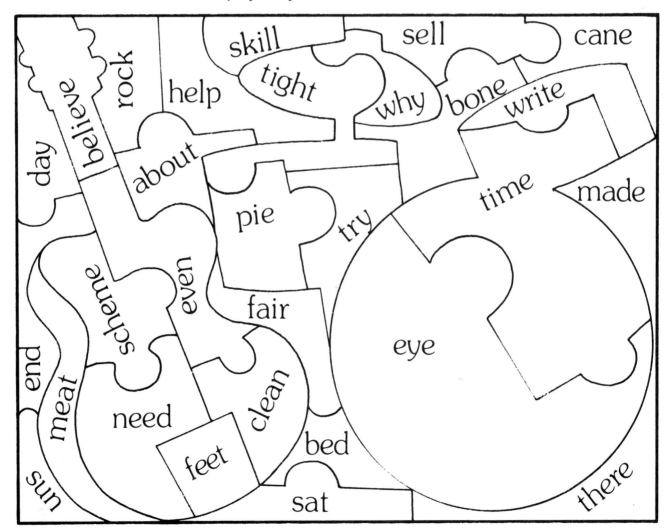

February 8   Name _____

Boy Scouts of America

Today is the birthday of the Boy Scouts of America. This organization for boys was started in 1910 by William Boyce. He got the idea from England, where he had been helped by a scout when he was lost in the fog. The group's motto is "Be prepared," and scouts believe in learning by doing. They must pass tests of skill and knowledge to earn merit badges. To earn a merit badge for first aid, for example, a scout must know such things as what to do in an emergency, how to give mouth-to-mouth resuscitation, and be able to make a sling and all kinds of bandages.

One of the requirements for a merit badge for citizenship in the community is to describe your town to a scout from another state or province. Write four sentences to describe your town or city. Tell about its industry, schools, religious buildings, ethnic groups, culture, and sports.

_____

_____

_____

_____

_____

_____

173

February 9

Name _____

New Idea Week

This is a good week for finding a new idea that will improve our surroundings. It can be a way to make a home more attractive, a school more interesting, a workplace more comfortable.

Spend 10 minutes right now and think of one way to make your classroom more interesting or comfortable or easier to work in. Try to think of some idea that does not take a lot of time or money. Write your idea here. Share it with your teacher.

My idea is _____

_____

_____

_____

February 10

Name _____

First Singing Telegram

In 1933 people could begin to send special kinds of telegrams. If someone wanted to wish a friend happy birthday, a person hired by the telegraph company would go to that friend's home and sing "Happy Birthday." You can still send singing telegrams today, but most of them are delivered by telephone.

Pretend the telegraph company will deliver these songs to friends or relatives of yours. Write down a time of year or a reason why you send each one. The first one is done.

"Listen to the Mockingbird"—to an aunt who is a birdwatcher

"Happy Birthday"—_____

"Let Me Call You Sweetheart"—_____

"Seventy-Six Trombones"—_____

"St. Patrick Was a Gentleman"—_____

"You're a Grand Old Flag"—_____

"My Dreidl"—_____

"Ten Little Goblins"—_____

"America"—_____

175

February 11

Name_____

Thomas Edison's Birthday

This great inventor was born in 1842. During his life he received more than 1,000 patents for new inventions or for improvements on old ones. His inventions included the light bulb, phonograph, and electric power station. He always tried to invent things that he thought people needed or wanted, that would work under ordinary conditions, would not easily get out of order, and would be simple to repair. Many people now observe his birthday as a day to honor all inventors.

Become an inventor today. But instead of machines, invent riddles about Edison's inventions. Write a riddle about the light bulb, then a second one about the phonograph. Take them home and see if you can stump your family.

_____

_____

_____

_____

_____

February 12

Name _____

Happy Birthday, Abe

Abraham Lincoln, our 16th president, was born in 1809. He is best remembered for being the president during the Civil War, for his Emancipation Proclamation that ended slavery, and for his Gettysburg Address.

Can you solve this cryptogram about Lincoln? Each number under the blanks below stands for a letter. The numbers that stand for the letters in Lincoln's name are given to you. Fill in the letters you know, then try to figure out what the others might be.

```
L  I  N  C  O  L  N
1  3  11 10 14 1  11     ‾ ‾ ‾ ‾ ‾    ‾ ‾ ‾    ‾ ‾    ‾ ‾ ‾ ‾    ‾ ‾ ‾ ‾ ‾
                         1 3 5 7 9    3 11     13     1 14 2     10 13 15 3 11

‾ ‾ ‾ ‾    ‾ ‾    ‾ ‾ ‾ ‾    ‾ ‾    ‾ ‾ ‾ ‾ ‾ .
8 6 7 11   6 7    8 13 4     13     10 6 3 1 9
```

February 13

Name _____

First Magazine in United States

American Magazine was the name of the first magazine published in America, in 1741. It beat, by about three days, a magazine published by Benjamin Franklin. *American Magazine* had 50 pages but appeared monthly for only three months. Franklin's publication did better. It became the forerunner of the *Saturday Evening Post*, still published today.

Make a survey of the magazines in your classroom. How many different ones are there?

_____

List the names of three of them and tell the kinds of stories or other information they contain.

1. _____ : _____

_____

2. _____ : _____

_____

3. _____ : _____

February 14

Name _____

Valentine's Day

No one really knows how Valentine's Day began, but people have been celebrating it for over 600 years. At first people sang or recited verses to each other. Today they usually send cards.

Color and cut out these pieces to make a valentine to give a friend. Or use some of the pieces to design your own card.

February 15   Name_____

Susan B. Anthony

Born in 1820, Susan B. Anthony spent her life working for laws to give women the right to vote. In 1872 she walked into a voting booth and voted, even though women were not allowed to vote. She was promptly arrested. But a hundred years later, in 1979, the country honored her for her courage by putting her likeness on a dollar coin.

    This amendment to the Constitution was passed in 1920.

Amendment 19—Woman Suffrage

Section 1. The right of citizens of the United States to vote shall not be denied or abridged by the United States or by any state on account of sex.

Section 2. Congress shall have power to enforce this article by appropriate legislation.

Use your dictionary to find the meanings of these important words in the amendment.

suffrage—_____

citizen—_____

deny—_____

abridge—_____

enforce—_____

legislation—_____

February 16   Name _____

First Comic Strip

In 1896 the first comic strip appeared in a newspaper. It was first called *Hogan's Alley*, but later it was named *The Yellow Kid*. The main character wore a yellow nightshirt.

Create your own comic strip hero or heroine. Draw a story about him or her.

The name of my character is _____.

My character has a friend named _____.
The two of them get into all sorts of trouble. Draw a comic strip to show the steps in their latest adventure.

February 17

Name_____

René Laennec's Birthday

Every time you go to the doctor, he or she probably uses Dr. Laennec's invention to examine you. This French doctor, born in 1781, needed some kind of instrument that would pick up the sounds of the heart and lungs. He used a hollow wooden tube to make the first stethoscope.

Make a simple stethoscope from a paper cup and a soda straw. Turn the cup upside down, make a small slit in the bottom of the cup, and fit one end of the straw into the slit. Now hold the open end of the cup against a friend's chest and put the other end of the straw to your ear. You should be able to hear your friend's heartbeats.

February 18

Name_____

Discovery of Pluto

For over one hundred years, astronomers had been looking for this planet. The unusual way that its neighboring planets moved had made them think there must be another planet out there. Finally, in 1930, two photographs of the sky taken a week apart showed that a faint point had moved its position. This tiny point of light was the missing planet, and it was called Pluto. Pluto is a small, cold planet. Its day is equal to about 6.5 earth days and its year is 284.4 earth years. It is the farthest planet from the sun.

Here is the order of the planets, starting with the one closest to the sun—Mercury, Venus, Earth, Mars, Jupiter, Saturn, Uranus, Neptune, Pluto.

To help you remember them in this order, make up a sentence with words that begin with the first letter of the planets' names. Keep them in the correct order. Here's a sample sentence. "Monday Vera Ellen Made John Stand Under Nancy's Plant." It doesn't have to make sense, just be easy to remember.

_____

_____

_____

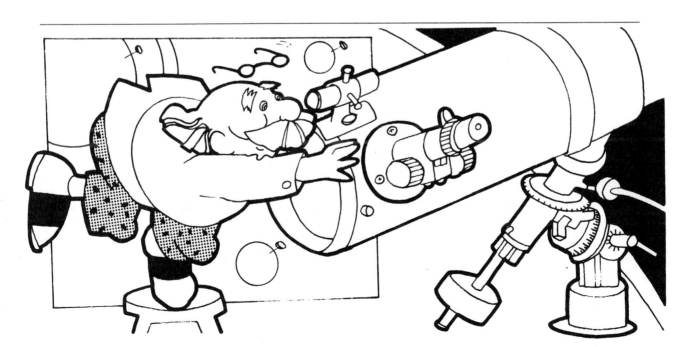

February 19

Name_____

Brotherhood Week

The week in which Washington's birthday falls is called Brotherhood Week. It is a time to learn about and understand other people and other ways of life. Brotherhood means acting or being like a brother. Act like a brother to some person this week.

Is there a boy or girl in your class you don't know very well? Ask your teacher if you can ask that person these questions. Write his or her answers here.

1. What is your name? _____

2. Do you have any brothers? _____

    Tell their names. _____

3. Do you have any sisters? _____

    Tell their names. _____

4. What is your favorite sport? _____
   _____

5. What would you like to know about me? _____
   _____
   _____
   _____

February 20

Name_____

Black History Month

February is Black History Month. In this month Abraham Lincoln was born, and on this day, in 1895, Frederick Douglass died. Mr. Douglass was born a slave in about 1817. He became a writer, speaker, and owner of a newspaper. He spent his life working for the end of slavery and for equal rights for black people.

Many black people have devoted their lives to helping their people. Can you match these names with their achievements? Use an encyclopedia if you need to.

Sojourner Truth	Editor of newspaper against slavery
W. E. B. DuBois	President of Bethune-Cookman College
Frederick Douglass	Led many slaves to safety in Canada
Harriet Tubman	Great woman speaker against slavery
Booker T. Washington	Started Tuskegee Institute school
Mary Bethune	Started National Association for the Advancement of Colored People

February 21

Name_____

First Telephone Directory

People who had telephones in Hew Haven, Connecticut, in 1878 got something new on this day— a directory that listed everyone's phone number. It was the first telephone directory ever and had only about 50 names. That was as many homes or businesses in the whole city that had telephones.

Start your own directory of telephone numbers. List names of friends and their phone numbers below. Take it home. Then the next time you want to call a friend you will have the number handy.

MY TELEPHONE DIRECTORY	
Name	Number
_____	_____
_____	_____
_____	_____
_____	_____
_____	_____
_____	_____
_____	_____
_____	_____
_____	_____

February 22   Name _____

Happy, Birthday, George Washington

Probably everyone in the United States knows the name of this man, born in 1732. He was the commander in chief of the American army during the war for independence and the country's first president. He is often called the father of his country. Probably no one else has so many towns, cities, mountains, and other places named after him. At least 30 states have a Washington County and almost as many have a town called Washington.

Use the atlas in your classroom, or borrow one, to see if there is something named Washington in your state. Write its name here and tell what it is.

_____   _____

Write down three other Washingtons from neighboring states and tell what they are.

_____   _____

_____   _____

February 23

Name _____

Polio Vaccine First Used

If you had been in school in Pittsburgh, Pennsylvania, on this day in 1954, you would probably have had to line up in front of the nurse's office for a shot. This was the day Pittsburgh schools began giving inoculations of vaccine to prevent polio. At last something had been created to keep people from getting this terrible disease.

Today boys and girls receive inoculations against many serious diseases. Rearrange the letters below to tell what diseases can be prevented if people have the correct vaccine.

lessmae   _____

spumm   _____

iloop   _____

slmal xpo   _____

bussuoiltrec _____

Take this page home to remind your parents that it is important to be inoculated. If you have not had all your shots, try to get them soon.

February 24

Name _____

First Rocket into Space

In 1949 a two-stage rocket was fired from White Sands Proving Grounds, New Mexico. It reached an altitude of 250 miles, the first U.S. rocket to reach outer space. Since then, space vehicles have gone much, much higher.

Write down these space flights in the column labeled "Flight," in the order they are given. Then plot the distance each flight went on the graph.

        Alan Shepard—116½ miles
        First rocket—250 miles
        Explorer VI, which took earth photos from space—19,500 miles
        Moon landings—250,000 miles
        Space probe to Venus—25,000,000 miles
        Space probe to Mars—35,000,000 miles

Flight	100	1,000	10,000	100,000	1,000,000	10,000,000	100,000,000
_____							
_____							
_____							
_____							
_____							
_____							

Miles away from earth

February 25

Name_____

New York to New Jersey Tunnel

In 1908 the first tunnel under the Hudson River was officially opened. It carried trains from Morton Street in New York City to Jersey City, New Jersey. The two tubes of the tunnel, one for each direction of traffic, were called the North or Uptown Tunnels. Today nine more tunnels connect New York City and New Jersey. They are used for railroad, subway, and automobile traffic.

Follow this tunnel from city to city. Start with Boston. In the next space, put a city or town that begins with N (the last letter in "Boston"), for example, Norfolk; then add a city or town that begins with the last letter of *that* city, and so on. Use an atlas to find city names if you need to. Continue until you reach the last space. What city is at the end of the tunnel?

February 26

Name _____

Buffalo Bill's Birthday

William D. Cody was born on this day in 1846. When he was a young man he killed buffaloes to supply meat to the men building the railroad across Kansas. He was such a good hunter people called him Buffalo Bill. In 1883 he organized a traveling show called the Wild West, Rocky Mountain and Prairie Exhibition. It traveled all over the United States and Europe. Thousands of people who had never seen Indians or cowboys came to watch them show their skills.

Perform your own skills with Buffalo Bill's name. See how many words you can make that end in ll. There are at least six words ending in ll that use only the letters in his name. Can you find them? You can also use different letters to make your list longer.

_____ ll   _____ ll   _____ ll

_____ ll   _____ ll   _____ ll

_____ ll   _____ ll   _____ ll

_____

February 27 Name_____

Longfellow Born

Henry Wadsworth Longfellow, born in 1807, was a well-known poet of the 1800s. Some of his poems, called narrative poems, tell long stories. One of them is called "The Song of Hiawatha." It is the story of an Indian boy and his experiences as he grows up and becomes an adult. In these lines Longfellow painted a word picture of Hiawatha and his animal friends.

> Of all beasts he learned the language,
> Learned their names and all their secrets,
> How the beavers built their lodges,
> Where the squirrels hid their acorns,
> How the reindeer ran so swiftly,
> Why the rabbit was so timid,
> Talked with them whene'er he met them,
> Called them "Hiawatha's Brothers."

Use your crayons to make a picture showing Hiawatha and some of his animal friends.

February 28

Name _____

Last M*A*S*H Show

This date in 1983 saw the final installment of this long-running TV program. M*A*S*H stands for Mobile Army Surgical Hospital. The program is the story of the activities at one of these mobile hospital units during the Korean War. The actual war went on for three years, from June 1950 to July 1953. The TV program ran more than three times that long, and old programs are still being shown today.

Answer these questions about your favorite TV program.
What is your favorite TV program? _____

What is it about? _____
_____

When is it televised? _____

On what channel? _____

On what network? _____

Why do you enjoy it? _____
_____

February 29

Name_____

Leap Year

Once every four years, we have leap year. Do you know why? It takes the earth just a few hours more than 365 days to go completely around the sun. In four years these few hours make about an extra day, which is added to February. A leap year is any year that can be divided evenly by four, except the years that are even hundreds, like 1900. An even-hundred year is a leap year if it can be divided evenly by 400.

Which of these years were or will be leap years? Put a Y for yes in front of each year below that is a leap year.

____ 1492   ____ 1809   ____ 1932

____ 1601   ____ 1886   ____ 1984

____ 1732   ____ 1904   ____ 2000

____ 1776   ____ 1927   ____ 2022

Chapter 3

Reproducibles for Spring

This group of spring reproducibles covers March 1 through June 20. *First Day of Spring, First Day of Summer,* and *Easter* are included in Chapter 4. Mother's Day (May 10) and Father's Day (June 19) are discussed on the days they were first observed.

Some of the late June pages will help you end the school year with a light touch—*Smile Power Day, National Hollerin' Contest, International Picnic Day, Ice Cream Soda Invented.* Creating sodas in class might be the perfect way to end the year!

March 1

Name _____

Our First National Park

In 1872 the United States created its first national park. It was Yellowstone National Park, a place of beautiful mountains, geysers, lakes, and waterfalls. Today the country has nearly 300 parklands for us to use and enjoy. Not all of them are actual parks. Some are monuments, like the Statue of Liberty. Some are historic places such as battlefields or homes of important Americans. Some are recreation places—seashores, lakes, and hunting areas. Every state except Delaware has at least one parkland.

Here are the names of some of our national parks. Tell what each one is famous for. Their names will give a clue.

Grand Canyon National Park _____

Carlsbad Caverns National Park _____

Crater Lake National Park _____

Petrified Forest National Park _____

Sequoia National Park _____

Mammoth Cave National Park _____

Great Smoky Mountains National Park _____

Glacier National Park _____

March 2   Name _____

Roads Get Numbers

Imagine getting directions like this for driving to a nearby city. "Go up West Hill, past the pond. Drive until you reach a yellow barn. Turn left, go through the woods, over a bridge, and past the lumber mill. Turn left again." Directions like these might get you where you're going sometimes. But what happened if the farmer painted his barn red, or the lumber mill closed down and was taken away? You'd need a more dependable way of finding your city.

On this day in 1925, the United States began using a system of route numbers to help automobile drivers get from place to place. Route numbers follow a special plan. U.S. roads and interstate highways have even numbers on roads going east and west. Roads going north and south have odd numbers. The lowest U.S. road numbers are in the North and East. The lowest interstate numbers are in the South and West.

Use an atlas, if you need to, to answer these questions.
What would be a good number for a U.S. interstate highway between:

1. Seattle, Washington, and Los Angeles, California? _____

2. Buffalo, New York, and Indianapolis, Indiana? _____

3. Duluth, Minnesota, and St. Louis, Missouri? _____

What would be a good number for a regular U.S. road between:

1. Santa Fe, New Mexico, and New Orleans, Louisiana? _____

2. Daytona Beach, Florida, and Pittsburgh, Pennsylvania? _____

3. Denver, Colorado, and Kansas City, Missouri? _____

March 3   Name_____

Watch for the Mail Carrier

On this day in 1863, the United States agreed to deliver mail to homes in large cities. Four hundred forty mail carriers were hired to deliver mail in 49 cities.

Sorting mail takes a lot of time. But ZIP codes help. ZIP means Zoning Improvement Plan. Here's how it works. The country is divided into 10 areas. The first ZIP code number stands for one of these areas. The 0 stands for the most eastern states, the 9 for those farthest west. In each area there are sectional centers that receive and sort the mail for the surrounding towns. The second and third ZIP numbers tell which sectional center a letter should go to. The last two numbers are for the town or part of a large city where the letter is being sent. The ZIP code 14221 goes to the area of New York, Pennsylvania, and Delaware (1), to the sectional center at Buffalo, New York (42), and to the suburb of Williamsville (21). ZIP code 63957 goes to the area of Illinois, Missouri, Kansas, and Nebraska (6), to the Poplar Bluff, Missouri, sectional center (39), then to the town of Piedmont (57).

What is your ZIP code?_____

Take a survey in your class. Does anyone have a different ZIP code? _____

What is it? _____

Ask to go to the office to find the ZIP code of your school. _____

Find a magazine. It doesn't matter which one. Look through the ads to find one ZIP code for each area 0 to 9.

0 _____   3 _____   6 _____

1 _____   4 _____   7 _____

2 _____   5 _____   8 _____

                                                                                                    9 _____

March 4

Name _____

President Caught Cold

This was the day, in 1841, when William Henry Harrison was inaugurated as 9th president of the United States. It was a cold, rainy day, but he refused to wear a hat at the outdoor ceremony. He caught a severe cold and never recovered. Thirty days later he died, the first president to die in office.

The United States Congress passed a law in 1886 that listed the persons who would take over in case a president or vice-president could not serve. They are the members of the president's cabinet, a group of advisers who work with him. This is the order in which cabinet members would move up to be president.

President _____

Vice-president _____

Secretary of State _____

Secretary of Treasury _____

Secretary of Defense _____

Attorney General _____

Secretary of Interior _____

Secretary of Agriculture _____

Secretary of Commerce _____

Secretary of Labor _____

Secretary of Health and Human Services _____

Secretary of Housing and Urban Development _____

Secretary of Transportation _____

Secretary of Energy _____ Secretary of Education _____

Write the names of the president and vice-president on the top two lines above. Can you find the names of any of the president's cabinet members?

March 5   Name_____

Youth Art Month

This is Youth Art Month. Make it a special month for trying some new kinds of art and craft activities.

Ask your teacher for six scraps of colored paper. Pick what colors you like. Use these scraps to make an interesting design. Tear the scraps into smaller shapes or just use them as you got them. Arrange them on this page. When you are happy with your arrangement, glue down the pieces.

March 6

Name _____

Iditarod Trail Race

A race that is over one thousand miles long? Yes, that's how far teams of dogsleds run each year in Alaska's Iditarod Trail Race. Fifty drivers and sleds and several hundred dogs leave Anchorage to race 1,049 miles to Nome. The winners get there just in time to enjoy the Nome winter carnival in March.

In some places of the world, dog sledding is still a common way to travel. Think for a minute about other ways people travel. Now look at the clock. Time yourself. List all the ways to travel you can think of in three minutes. Get ready, get set, go!!

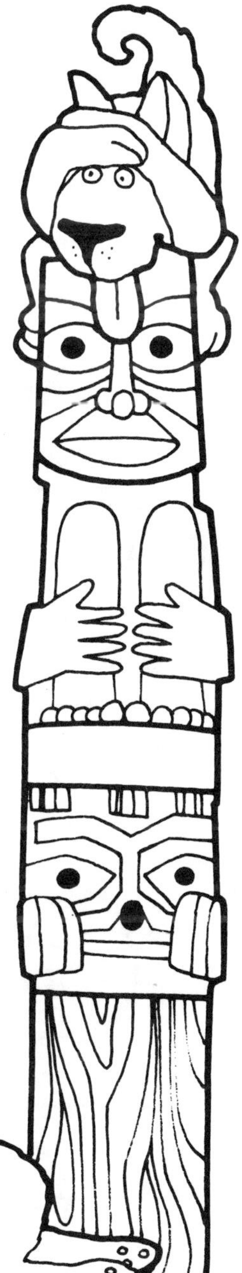

March 7

Name _____

Birthday of Luther Burbank

This man, born in 1849, was a horticulturist. A horticulturist is someone who is skilled in growing fruits, vegetables, flowers, and ornamental plants. Mr. Burbank would select only the strongest and best plants to grow. When the plants had seeds, he would keep only the best ones. He managed to create many new plants. An example is the plumcot, which is half plum, half apricot. A potato he created is called the Burbank potato.

Become a horticulturist yourself. Fill a small pot with soil. You can use a plastic cottage cheese container. Plant five or six seeds. Use any kind. If you have a bird feeder, it might be fun to plant a few bird seeds. When the seeds come up, keep only the strongest one and cut off the rest. Water it carefully. When it has grown, take it home as a spring gift for someone.

March 8   Name _____

A First Dog License

Do you have a pet dog? Does it have a license? The first dog license law in the United States was passed in New York State on March 8, 1894. It said that anyone living in a city with over 1,200,000 people and who owned a dog had to pay $2.00 each year. At that time, the only city in the state with that many people was New York City. No one outside of the city had to buy a license. A license gives you permission to own something (dog), to use something (car), or to do some special thing (drive a car).

What kinds of licenses do you know about? List as many as you can here. You and a friend might work together to make a long list.

_____ _____

_____ _____

_____ _____

_____ _____

_____ _____

March 9

Name _____

Hurray for Amerigo!

Citizens of North and South America should remember this day. It is the birthday of Amerigo Vespucci, born in 1451. He was a pilot on a ship that explored the coast of South America in 1497. When he got home, he claimed he had discovered a new continent and wrote letters telling about it. The letters were published. In 1507 someone suggested the continent be called America "because Amerigo discovered it." Today we know his ship was not the first to reach South America, but his name lives on because he wrote about it.

There were many early explorers of this part of the world. We have honored some of them by naming natural or man-made spots after them. Write down one place named for each of these people. If you have trouble, an atlas will help you.

Henry Hudson _____

Amerigo Vespucci _____

Christopher Columbus _____

Vitus Bering _____

Ferdinand Magellan _____

George Vancouver _____

Giovanni da Verrazano _____

James Cook _____

March 10

Name _____

First Telephone Message

On this day in 1876, Alexander Graham Bell made the first telephone call. He was working on his invention and used it to call his helper in another room. He said, "Mr. Watson, come here. I want you." Mr. Watson heard him through the machine.

Do you know how a telephone works? When you speak into a telephone, the sounds of your voice make a thin metal disk, which is called a diaphragm, vibrate. The vibrations regulate some electric currents that are then sent through wires to the telephone of the person you're speaking to.

You can make a simple telephone with two empty tin cans and string. Cut off the tops of the cans and punch a small hole in the bottom of each one. Connect the cans, with the open ends facing outward, by putting a piece of cotton string through the holes. Tie knots on the ends of the string to hold it in place. Now give a friend one can to hold while you hold the other. Keep the string tight and in a straight line. Speak into the open end of your can. The vibrations will go along the string until they reach the other can. By putting his or her ear to the open end of the second can, your friend will hear what you are saying.

March 11

Name _____

Great Blizzard of '88

We think of March as the time of the coming of spring, but there was no spring in the eastern United States on March 11, 1888. The snow and wind began in the evening and by the time it ended on March 14, drifts 30 feet high had covered parts of New York City. This was a freak storm, and there hasn't been one like it since then. But each year severe storms hit some part of the world.

The most common types of bad storms and other natural disasters are listed here. Using your dictionary, tell what each one is.

blizzard— _____

_____

tornado— _____

_____

hurricane— _____

_____

tidal wave— _____

_____

earthquake— _____

_____

typhoon— _____

_____

March 12

Name _____

Girl Scouts in America

On this day in 1912, the first Girl Scout troop meeting was held. Mrs. Juliette Gordon Low started the troop in Savannah, Georgia. She took the idea from the Girl Guides, which began in England in 1909. The Girl Guides in Canada, started in 1910, are similar to the Girl Scouts in the United States.

Help these scouts hike to the top of the mountain. Start at the campsite and try to reach the peak without crossing any lines. Can you find the one path that goes to the top?

March 13   Name_____

A Patent for Earmuffs

On March 13, 1877, Chester Greenwood received a patent for his invention. This man from Maine had invented "ear mufflers" to protect ears in the cold Maine winters. Many other people have invented pieces of clothing or equipment for people who live in cold, wintery climates. A few of these inventions are snowmobiles, ski masks, and leg warmers.

Can you invent something for people who live where the climate is unusual? It might be a nose warmer for cold winters, an umbrella with a window for very rainy places, or a jacket filled with ice cubes for hot, desert areas. Draw a picture of your invention and then tell how it works.

March 14   Name _____

Happy Birthday, Camp Fire Girls

This is the week to help the Camp Fire Girls celebrate their birthday. This organization began in Maine in 1910. Camp Fire Girls enjoy crafts, outdoor sports, camping, music, helping others, doing conservation projects, and other interesting activities. Their watchword is *wohelo*. It is made from the first two letters of work, health, and love. Its symbol is two crossed logs and a flame, to remind members of the warmth of home and the wonder of outdoors.

Think about a club it would be fun to belong to. Decide what members would do and pick a name for it. Then design a symbol or a watchword for the club. Here are some club ideas, but you can probably think of better ones: Mystery Readers (read and discuss mystery books), Model Makers (make model airplanes, ships, cars), Racers (race toy cars), Green Thumbers (grow flowers or vegetables in a garden or window box).

My club would be called _____

Its members would _____

_____

Its watchword would be _____

Its symbol would look like this:

March 15

Name _____

Welcome Back, Buzzards

Each year on this day, buzzards begin to return from their winter homes to Hinckley, Ohio, to make their nests. A celebration is held in this small town to welcome them back. Some people think these buzzards, or turkey vultures, are ugly, with their small red heads and hooked bills. But they are valuable to us. They use their keen eyes to see dead animals. Then they get rid of these animals by eating them. If the dead animals were left to decay, they would make the land pretty unhealthy.

Practice measuring to scale, using a ruler or measuring tape. If ½ inch equals one foot, what is the size and wing span of these birds?

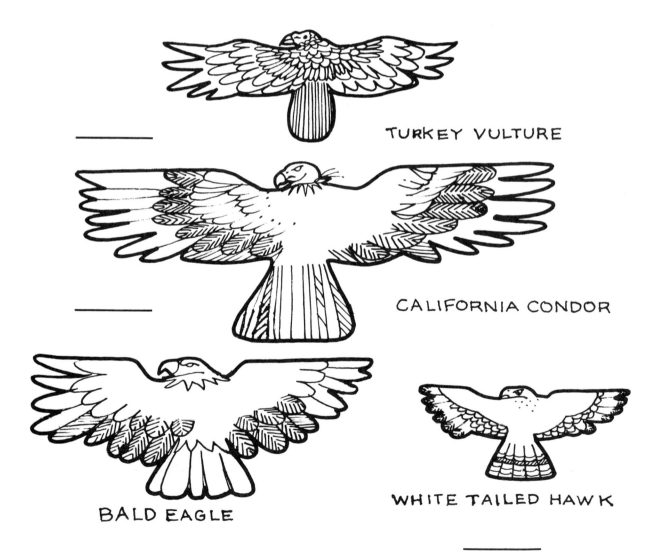

March 16

Name_____

Docking Day

Today in 1966, two spaceships orbited earth, then met and were docked together. Can you imagine how complicated it must have been to plan their flights from earth so accurately that they could meet perfectly?

Try this simple experiment with a friend. Each of you must get a paper cup. Face your friend, and hold the cups so the open ends fit exactly together. Now, keeping your arms in those exact positions, turn around so you and your friend are back to back. Both of you walk in a kind of half circle until you meet again, as this diagram shows. Don't cheat. Don't adjust the cups. Just try to keep them as they were when you started. When you come together again, do your cups meet exactly? Think about the problems Neil Armstrong and David Scott must have had with their spaceships out in space.

211

March 17

Name _____

St. Patrick's Day

This is the day when the people of Ireland and Northern Ireland honor St. Patrick. This missionary spent 30 years in Ireland, where he talked to people about Christ and started 300 churches. Parades and parties help people celebrate St. Patrick's Day. Irish people who live in other countries also enjoy this day.

Many things we use or enjoy have some connection with Ireland, so the word "Irish" is part of their name. Here are some definitions. Complete their names at the right.

Vegetable we can bake or mash	Irish _____
Kind of dog	Irish _____
Loose open cloth to decorate clothing	Irish _____
Food of lamb, potatoes, onions	Irish _____
Lively dance	Irish _____
Woolen cloth woven in a special way	Irish _____

March 18   Name _____

Red Cross Month

March is Red Cross Month. The Red Cross works to help people in times of war, natural disaster, or any kind of trouble. Most of the members of the Red Cross are volunteers who work without pay. The Red Cross collects blood which is given to hospitals. It gives classes in first aid, lifesaving, swimming, good health, and child care. It helps people in the armed forces. It helps war veterans get benefits or hospital care. It gives food and shelter to people who have lost homes in floods, fires, earthquakes, tornadoes, and hurricanes.

Use the facts given above to write eight sentences or descriptions about the Red Cross. Start each sentence with one of the letters in *Red Cross*. The first one is done for you.

R eady to help in times of trouble

E _____

D _____

C _____

R _____

O _____

S _____

S _____

March 19

Name _____

National Wildlife Week

The National Wildlife Federation wants people to get outdoors this week and enjoy the beauty and freedom of wildlife. Sometime this week, take a long walk in a nearby park, or to a wooded area. Sit quietly and listen and look for animals, birds, and insects. You will be surprised how many will come close to you if you are very quiet and still.

With several friends, make a classroom mural of the wildlife in your area. Even if you live in a city, you can find many animals, insects, and birds. Make drawings of them, then color and cut them out. Mount on a long strip of newsprint or shelf paper. Add scenery with crayons. Be sure you put each animal in the proper place—birds in the air, frogs in or near a pond, a woodchuck near the mouth of its burrow.

March 20

Name _____

Poison Prevention Week

This is a very important week. It is a time to make sure no one in your house ever uses any kind of poison by mistake. A lot of things in our homes are poisonous. Many products that make clothes cleaner or open clogged drains are dangerous to drink or even smell. Medicines that make some people well are poisonous for other people. Even parts of some garden flowers are poisonous to eat. A skull and crossbones is a symbol of something poisonous. If you see that on a container, you know that what's inside the container is dangerous.

Design your own symbol to warn about poisons. Make it big and bright. Draw several copies of your design and cut them out. Take them home and ask your mother or father if you can tape one on every box or bottle that has poisonous materials. Then tell your younger brothers and sisters to leave such things alone.

Do two more things. Put all the poisonous things in your house on high shelves. Look in the front of your telephone directory for the number of the poison control center near you. Write it on a piece of paper and tape it near the telephone. If you ever need to call, the number will be handy.

March 21

Name _____

Earth Day

The first International Earth Day was observed in April, 1970. Now it is celebrated on the first day of spring. Earth Day is a time to think of ways to save water, trees, metals, and other natural resources. Every time we use a scrap of paper instead of a new sheet of paper, we help save a tree. Every aluminum can we take to a recycling plant protects our supply of aluminum ore.

Be an Earth Day booster. Color this badge. Cut it out and mount it on cardboard. Pin it to your shirt or blouse so everyone knows you are doing your part to save the earth's resources.

Be an Earth Day booster in another way by doing at least three of these things. Check the ones you will do.

_____ I will use both sides of my writing paper.

_____ I will eat all my lunch.

_____ I will turn off lights when leaving the room.

_____ I will make sure all water faucets are turned off tightly.

_____ I will return all bottles or cans.

_____ I will not harm small trees or break off tree branches.

_____ I will not dig up grass or flowers.

March 22

Name_____

National Goof-Off Day

Everyone needs one special day each year just to goof off. Today is the day! It is a day for fun and silliness. But remember, you are only allowed one goof-off day a year. No more for the rest of the year. Or maybe you've already had your goof-off day. In that case, forget this one and let someone else read these elephant riddles!

How do you make an elephant float?
Put 1 elephant, 2 scoops of ice cream, and some soda water in a very, very large glass.

How can you tell if there is an elephant sleeping in your bed?
Look for peanut shells.

How do you fit 5 elephants in a Volkswagen?
Put 2 in the front, 2 in the back, and 1 in the glove compartment.

Why did the elephant paint itself different colors?
So it could hide in the crayon box.

What time is it when an elephant sits on a fence?
Time to build a new fence.

Why did the elephant wear sunglasses?
With all the silly elephant riddles going around, it didn't want to be recognized.

March 23

Name _____

Going Up!

On this day in 1857, customers at the Haughwout Department Store in New York City could ride from the first to the fifth floors. Elisha Graves Otis had installed the first elevator that would carry passengers to an upper floor of a building. It made the trip in less than a minute. This seemed pretty fast. But today you can take an elevator to the 103rd floor of the Sears Tower in Chicago in the same length of time!

Ride the elevator to the top of this building. Start with 1 on the first floor, add 2 for the second floor, then keep adding the number of each floor to your total until you reach the tenth floor.

_ + 10 =

_ + 9 =

_ + 8 =

_ + 7 =

_ + 6 =

_ + 5 =

_ + 4 =

_ + 3 =

1 + 2 =

If you are really ambitious, you might try to multiply the numbers. With a calculator you'll have no trouble at all.

March 24

Name _____

Birthday of John Wesley Powell

Born this day in 1834, John Wesley Powell was one of the first persons to see the Grand Canyon, from the bottom. In 1869 this one-armed college professor led a boat expedition for 1,000 miles on the Colorado River. The trip was 101 days long and took the group through the length of the Grand Canyon. Mr. Powell was a geologist. A geologist is a person who studies the history of the earth by exploring its rocks.

Solve these math problems about Mr. Powell's trip.

1. How old was Mr. Powell when he explored the Colorado River? _____

2. If the trip started on May 24, when did it end? _____

3. About how many miles must the group have traveled each day? _____

4. About how many weeks long was the trip? _____

5. About how many months? _____

6. The Grand Canyon is about 215 miles long. How many miles of the trip were not through the canyon? _____

March 25

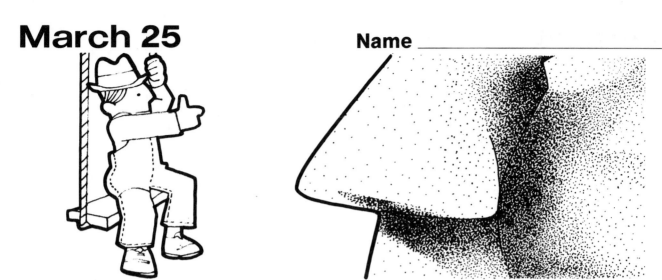

Gutzon Borglum Born

The name of this American sculptor, born in 1871, is not very well known. But you probably have seen many pictures of his most important project. The Mt. Rushmore National Memorial in South Dakota was his idea. He planned the faces and supervised most of the work in carving them. We can thank him for this special memorial to four great presidents—Washington, Jefferson, Lincoln and T. Roosevelt.

If two more presidents were to be added to Mt. Rushmore, which two would be your candidates? Write their names here and tell why they should be added. Use your social studies book or an encyclopedia for help.

I would add President _____ because _____

_____

_____

I would add President _____ because _____

_____

_____

March 26   Name_____

Hurray for Popeye!

What is Popeye's favorite food? Spinach! The spinach growers of Texas were so happy about it that they put up a Popeye statue. The six-foot-tall statue appeared during their spinach festival in 1937, in Crystal City, Texas. It was made of concrete and painted to look just like him.

Make your own statue. From clay or any modeling material mold a favorite comic strip person or animal. You could do Popeye, Mickey Mouse, Snoopy, good old Charlie Brown, or any one you wish.

Birthday of Wilhelm Konrad Roentgen

This German scientist, born in 1845, discovered that certain invisible rays would pass through some things, but not through others. They would go through flesh but not bones. He used these rays to photograph the bones of his hand. *X* is a science term for something unknown. Since Mr. Roentgen did not know what the rays were, he called them X. X rays can be dangerous if not used correctly. But the careful use of X rays helps people learn many things.

Doctors can find broken bones.
Dentists can see hidden cavities.
Metal workers can notice hidden cracks in certain metals.
Archaeologists can find old treasures under dirt or rust.
Experts can find valuable art that has been covered by paint.
Airport officials can locate weapons in luggage.
X rays can burn and destroy cancer cells.
X rays can kill germs on surgical tools.

Complete this puzzle, using the underlined words above.

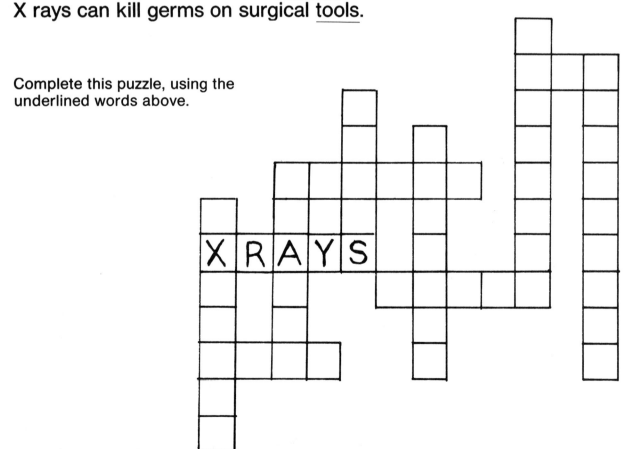

March 28

A First Subway

On this day in 1895, workers began digging America's first subway in Boston. Two years later, people started riding the subway on a track that was 1½ miles long. Today most of the largest cities in the world have subways.

The word subway is made up of two word parts. Sub is a prefix that means below or beneath or under. Way stands for highway or passageway.

Many other common words start with the prefix sub. What sub words can you think of for these definitions? Use a dictionary if you need to.

An underground tunnel is a _____.

A vehicle that travels underwater is a _____.

When we make a large field into small lots, we _____ it.

Something that is not as good as it should be is _____.

A small, undersize car is called a _____.

March 29

Name _____

Niagara Falls Didn't Fall

Every minute 500,000 tons of water rush over a cliff to create Niagara Falls. But on this day in 1848, no water went over the edge. Huge chunks of ice from Lake Erie had piled up in the river above the falls and held back all the water.

Pretend you are a TV news anchorman giving the evening news. Explain this most unusual event. Tell how less and less water went over the falls until finally there was none. Give the TV viewers a word picture of the dry cliffs. Finally, describe the great roar and rushing of ice and water as the ice dam broke. On the lines below make an outline of your report so you won't forget any details. If you can, tape-record your report, then play it back to yourself so you can hear how it sounds.

_____

_____

_____

_____

_____

_____

_____

_____

_____

_____

_____

March 30

Name _____

An Eraser at Last

Boys and girls found it easier to correct a mistake after this day in 1858. That's when Hyman L. Lipman of Philadelphia, Pennsylvania, received a patent for putting an eraser on the end of a pencil. The pencil had a groove at the top, into which was "secured a piece of prepared rubber, glued in at one end."

Did you know these facts about a pencil?

The "lead" in a pencil is not really lead, but a mixture of graphite, clay, wax, and chemicals. The more clay there is, the harder the lead.

The wooden part of most pencils is 7¼ inches long.

The eraser end is made of rubber. Rubber got its name because it was first used to "rub out" marks.

There's enough lead in a pencil to draw a line 35 miles long.

Look at the pencil you are using. Write the number stamped on it. _____ Is it hard or soft? _____ Find a pencil with a different number. Write the number here. _____ Is it harder or softer? _____

Can you find a third pencil with a different number? Write its number and tell if it is harder

_____

or softer than the first one. _____

Underline the correct word in this sentence: A pencil with a number 1 is (harder, softer) than a pencil with a number 4. _____

March 31

Name _____

Spring Ahead, Fall Back

On this day in 1918, the clocks in the United States were set ahead one hour. It gave everyone an extra hour of daylight in the evening. This was important because at that time World War I was being fought, and the country needed to save energy. When the war ended, so did daylight saving time. But since 1967, most of the country has again been using daylight saving time in the summer months. It begins on the last Sunday in April and ends on the last Sunday in October.

Underline the words that will make these sentences correct.
1. At 9:00 P.M. central standard time, David's mother changed the clocks to daylight saving time. She moved the hands to read (8:00, 10:00) P.M.
2. On the last Sunday in October, Margery forgot to change her watch and was (early, late) for Sunday school.
3. "Tomorrow daylight saving time starts," called Joe to Ruth. "Make sure you move your clock (ahead, back) one hour."
4. "I always remember the saying *Spring ahead, fall back*. That way I know which way to move my clock," she replied.

Tell what Ruth meant. _____

_____

226

April 1

Name _____

April Fools' Day

People have been observing this day for over 300 years. It all started in 1564, in France. France was the first country to begin to use a new calendar. In the old calendar the first month of the new year went from the beginning of spring to April 1. This new calendar started the new year in January. Some people still kept the old celebration. They were teased about it and were called April Fools.

Plan some April Fool tricks to play on your friends. Be sure your tricks are funny ones that will not harm anybody. Here are some ideas.
1. Tell someone a huge bug is crawling up his or her arm.
2. Address an envelope to look like a real letter. Give it to your Dad. Inside the envelope, put a piece of paper that says "April Fool."
3. In an excited voice tell someone an unusual animal is walking down the street and to come look.
4. Offer someone a stick of gum that is really an empty wrapper.
Write down the special trick you are planning.

_____

_____

_____

April 2

Name _____

The U.S. Mint

In 1792 the U.S. government agreed to create a mint, or factory, to make coins for the new country. The mint would be built in Philadelphia and would make gold, silver, and copper coins. The gold coins were called the eagle ($10), half eagle ($5), and quarter eagle ($2.50). Silver coins were the dollar, half dollar, quarter dollar, dime, and half dime. One-cent and half-cent coins were made from copper.

Celebrate this date with some rubbings of the coins we use today. Place a coin under this paper and rub across it with the side of a soft pencil or crayon.

April 3

Name _____

Washington Irving Born

Washington Irving, born today in 1783, was a writer who became famous in Europe as well as in the United States. He wrote long biographies of George Washington and Christopher Columbus. But boys and girls know him best for two stories about the Dutch settlers along the Hudson River. "Rip Van Winkle" is the story of a rather lazy man who wandered into the hills and fell asleep for 20 years. "The Legend of Sleepy Hollow" is about Ichabod Crane, who was chased by a "headless" horseman. If you haven't read these stories, ask for them at the library.

Imagine what it would be like to leave home one afternoon and not come back for 20 years. Make a list of all the things that would be different, such as much older friends and relatives, new buildings built and old ones torn down. What new inventions might have been made? Use your imagination. See how long a list you can make.

Flag Plan Set

When the U.S. flag was designed, it had 13 stripes and 13 stars, one for each of the first states. Then two new states were formed, and 2 stars and 2 stripes were added. By 1817 there were 20 states. It didn't seem possible to have a 20-stripe flag. Finally, on April 4, 1818, the United States Congress decided to "establish the flag of the United States with 13 stripes for the first 13 colonies and 20 stars for the states . . . with a star to be added" for each new state.

Today the flag has 50 stars—5 rows with 6 stars and 4 rows with 5 stars. Pretend a new state is being added to the country. Place 51 stars in a pleasing arrangement in this star field. You may want to practice on scrap paper first.

April 5   Name _____

Booker T. Washington

Born a slave in 1856, Booker T. Washington grew up to become an important leader and teacher of black people. He is best known as the founder of Tuskegee Institute, a school that teaches such skills as carpentry, farming, mechanics, and teaching. The first buildings at Tuskegee were an abandoned church and a shanty. On Sundays Washington would drive through the country, talking to young black people and urging them to come to school. Today Tuskegee Institute has about 4,000 students. It teaches such subjects as education, nursing, engineering, veterinary medicine, and science.

Help Washington recruit students. Using letters and pictures cut from newspapers and magazines, make a collage poster to advertise the importance of going to school.

First Modern Olympics

The very first Olympic game was held at the stadium of Olympia, Greece, in 776 B.C. It was a foot race about 200 yards long. Other games were added after that, but they stopped being played in A.D. 394. The stadium was destroyed and buried. When archaeologists uncovered it in 1875, a French educator got the idea of starting up the games again. A few years later his idea became a reality. The first modern Olympics began on this day in 1896, in Athens, Greece.

Olympic games have been held every four years since then except during world wars. Each time the games are held, a torch is lighted in the valley of Olympia, Greece, and carried to the country where the games are being played. Greek runners carry it to the border of Greece, then runners from each country it passes through carry it from there. Ships and planes carry it over oceans and mountains. The last runner enters the stadium, circles the track, and lights the flame.

The Olympic flag has five interlocking rings. They stand for the continents of Africa, Asia, Australia, Europe, and the Americas. Each ring is a different color—black, blue, green, red, and yellow. Flags of all competing nations contain at least one of these colors.

Use the underlined words above to complete this puzzle. On another sheet of paper, create your own puzzle for a friend to complete.

An Unusual Race

A race that never ended was held on this day in 1864. Several camels were lined up on an oval track in Sacramento, California. Men prodded and pushed the camels to start them around the track. At the first curve, they stopped to munch grass. The prodders went to work again. but not one camel ever finished the race.

Where did these animals come from? A few years before, the army had imported about 80 camels to carry supplies from Texas to California. But railroads were being built that were faster and cheaper, so most of the camels were sold or left to wander off in the desert. The racing camels were owned by a man who had bought several of these discarded creatures.

A camel is a very unusual animal, but many facts we hear about them are not true. Read these sentences. Before each put a T if it is true, an F if it is false. Check your answers with the encyclopedia.

_____ 1. A camel stores water in its hump.
_____ 2. A camel can kick with its hind legs.
_____ 3. Camels really need more water than people think because they perspire a lot.
_____ 4. A camel is a very disagreeable animal and often spits at people and other animals.
_____ 5. People eat the meat of camels.
_____ 6. Camel hair is woven into cloth and blankets.
_____ 7. A camel does not follow commands well because it cannot hear.
_____ 8. A person can get "seasick" riding on a camel because it sways as it walks.
_____ 9. A camel makes a friendly pet.

April 8

Name _____

A New Record

Wouldn't you like to have been in the Atlanta, Georgia, baseball stadium on this day in 1974? Imagine the excitement when Henry L. (Hank) Aaron hit his 715th home run. It broke a major league record of almost 40 years. In the next two years, Hank hit 40 more, for a total of 755 major league home runs.

When sports announcers talk about baseball batters, they give the players' batting averages. To find a person's batting average, you must divide the number of hits he makes by the number of times he bats. If someone gets 3 hits in 10 times at bat, he has a batting average of .300. This is very, very good. Use your calculator to see if these players are good batters. Put checks by the five best batters.

Name	Times at Bat	Number of Hits	Batting Average
J. Powers	399	134	_____
M. Smith	602	145	_____
R. Jones	416	133	_____
J. Dunn	361	88	_____
K. Thomas	501	90	_____
S. Dobbs	431	126	_____
F. Russell	355	101	_____
B. Wilson	521	130	_____

April 9

A New Word Is Born

A steamship docked in New York on April 9, 1882. A great iron box was lifted off by a derrick and drawn away by 16 horses. Inside was an elephant so huge that today we use its name to describe something very big. P. T. Barnum had purchased the elephant from the London Zoo to exhibit in his circus. It was 11 feet high and weighed 7½ tons. The end of its trunk could reach 26 feet into the air. The elephant's keeper had made up a word that he thought described something big. He called the elephant Jumbo. Whenever you see a jumbo-sized box of detergent, think of this great elephant.

Many other words came about in a similar way.

Gargantua was a huge, fictional king with a great appetite.

Small chickens lived on an island named Bantam.

In *Gulliver's Travels*, the hero was captured by tiny people who lived in Lilliput.

In the Old Testament, David killed Goliath, a very large man.

Stories of ancient Greece told about very big people who were called giants.

Use the facts above to write the meanings of these phrases:

bantam bowlers _____

gargantuan thirst _____

giant panda _____

lilliputian doll _____

a baseball Goliath _____

Patent for Safety Pin

When Walter Hunt got his idea on this day in 1948, he moved fast. In only three hours, he thought of an idea for a safety pin, made a model of it, and sold all his rights to it for $100. His invention is called the safety pin because a guard over the point makes it safer than other pins.

Many things we have and use have two words to their names. The first word describes the second one and tells us more about it. Sometimes both words are written together as one word. What word should be put first to complete these names of familiar things.

_____	chair	has runners so it can go back and forth
_____	boat	moves by wind
_____	stool	has one or two steps
_____	corn	explodes when heated
_____	glass	colored by something melted into it
_____	line	for hanging laundry on
_____	case	for holding books
_____	book	collection of recipes
_____	room	where we take a bath
_____	pot	for cooking a beverage

Now, you think of two similar kinds of names.

First Major League Black Player

A pioneer is a person who ventures into unknown territory or becomes involved in a new activity. The first settlers to this country were pioneers. The first person to fly was a pioneer. On this day in 1947, Jackie Robinson was a pioneer. He became the first black person to join a major league baseball team.

Here are some other pioneers. Match them up with the places or events that made them pioneers. If you have trouble, look them up in an encyclopedia.

Yuri Gargarin	First persons to fly
Neil Armstrong	First woman doctor in the United States
Zebulon Pike	First explorer to see Alaska
Norsemen	First person in space
Wright Brothers	First persons to land in North America
Elizabeth Blackwell	First black woman in the House of Representatives
Vitus Bering	First white person to discover Pikes Peak
Shirley Chisholm	First person to step on the moon

April 12   Name _____

First Space Shuttle Flight

This was an important day in 1981. The space shuttle *Columbia* made its first test flight. The *Columbia* is different from other space vehicles. It is a rocket that is projected into space but then can be flown back to earth like a conventional airplane and be used again and again. It is a working vehicle. On its later flights, it put satellites into orbit. One time it even rescued a satellite that was not working right, repaired it, and placed it back into its old orbit.

Do you know what the space shuttle looks like? Counting by 5s, connect the numbered dots. When you finish, you'll find a sketch of this important vehicle.

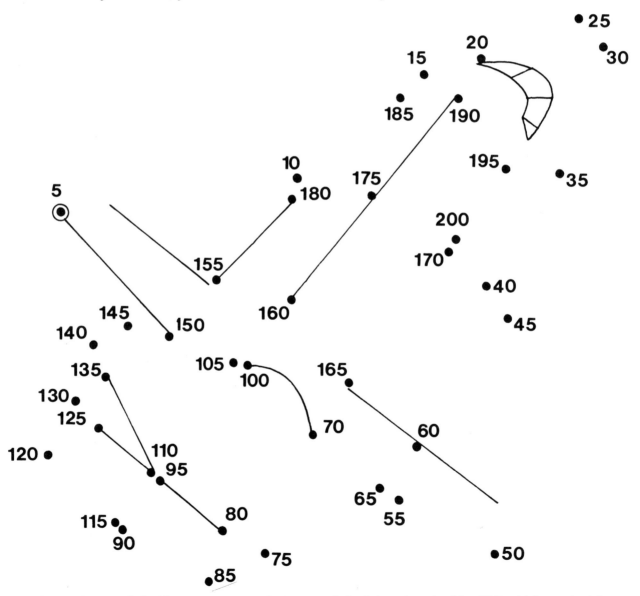

Model makers might like to put together a model of the shuttle. You'll find kits at hobby or craft stores.

April 13

Name _____

Thomas Jefferson Born

Thomas Jefferson was born in 1743. This great patriot is most remembered for writing the Declaration of Independence. But he studied law and was also an inventor, a musician, an architect, president, and diplomat. He was the first U.S. ambassador to France. He planned the buildings of the University of Virginia. He and his wife Martha lived in a large home in Virginia that he called Monticello.

Can you find the underlined words about Jefferson in the puzzle below? Words go up and down, backward and forward.

```
M O N T I C E L L O G
A W G O T M B N V F N
H R S D B U E H F J I
T X P R E S I D E N T
I C A P U I K O M N I
A W T Q E C N A R F R
J A R C H I T E C T W
B L I E K A A R L P T
D C O A I N I G R I V
A H T R A M D I L G M
```

April 14

Name _____

National Library Week

This is the week to think about the libraries in your town and school. Do you visit them often? Do you know what kinds of materials you can see and use there? Plan a trip to one of the libraries this week. If you do not have a library card, apply for one then.

Make a book jacket to illustrate and describe your favorite book. On the front, put the title, author, and some kind of drawing or design that shows a little bit of what the book is about. On the back, write two or three sentences describing the book and its author. Perhaps your class can display these original book jackets on the bulletin board.

April 15

Name_____

Largest Milkshake

If you had had 50¢ in Ithaca, New York, on April 15, 1984, you could have had a sample of the world's largest milkshake. It was one of the attractions at the dairy cow show and contained 77 gallons of ice cream.

Suppose you had been the chairman of the committee to make this milkshake. Solve these math problems.

1. If it takes 1 quart of ice cream to make shakes for 6 people, how many shakes can you make from 1 gallon?_____

2. How many people would 77 gallons serve?_____

3. If it takes 1 quart of milk to make 4 shakes, how many quarts are needed for 100 shakes?_____

4. For 1,000 shakes?_____

5. How many gallons is that?_____

6. How many gallons of milk were needed for the largest milkshake?_____

April 16

Name_____

National Humor Month

April is National Humor Month, a time to make neighbors, friends, and family laugh. Find a new joke each day and tell it each night around the dinner table.

What was the funniest thing that ever happened to you? Tell about it in a paragraph. Use interesting words so others will think it was funny, too.

_____

_____

_____

_____

_____

With your classmates, make a bulletin board. Cut out letters that say "A Funny Thing Happened!" Mount them on the board, then put everyone's paragraphs underneath the words for others to read.

April 17

Bicycle Safety Week

This is a week to think about bicycles and how to ride them safely. The first bicycles were imported from Europe in 1819. They had no pedals. People walked them along the street, and only rode them when they went downhill. They were called "swift walkers." About 20 years later, foot pedals were added to the front wheels. Rides on these bicycles were very bumpy, and people called them "bone shakers." Then a new type, called a high wheeler, was invented. It had a front wheel five feet high and a very small rear wheel. By about 1885, the bicycles looked much like those today. They had a chain, sprocket, and pedals that drove the rear wheels.

Do you have a bicycle? During this week, give it this safety check.

_____ 1. Are the tires in good condition?
_____ 2. Do they have the proper amount of air?
_____ 3. Does the bike have reflectors at the front and back and on the pedals?
_____ 4. Are the sidewalls of the tires reflective, or are there reflectors on the spokes?
_____ 5. Have you oiled it lately?
_____ 6. Are the brakes O.K.?
_____ 7. Do you have an up-to-date license?
_____ 8. Do you know all the rules for safe riding in your town?

April 18

Name _____

A Washateria

On this day in 1934, Mr. J.F. Cantrell started the first self-service laundry. He had four electric washing machines that he rented for an hour at a time. Users had to furnish their own soap and take the wet clothes home to hang up. He called his business a washateria. Later someone designed machines that did a load of washing for a certain number of coins. Places with these kinds of machines were called laundromats.

Create some new words like *washateria* and *laundromat*.

The suffix -teria means "a place having self-service." Start a list of self-service stores.

The suffix -omat means "an automatic operation, especially a store using coin-operated devices." Start a list of coin-operated stores.

Think about stores for buying gasoline, milk, ice cream, clothing, vegetables, toys; stores for playing video games, using exercise equipment, working with computers. Which ones could be self-service; which ones could provide products or services with coin-operated devices? Use your imagination, and add to the lists below.

-teria	-omat
washateria	laundromat
cafeteria	automat
_____	_____
_____	_____
_____	_____
_____	_____

April 19

Name _____

The Boston Marathon

An important Olympic game is a running race called the marathon. After the first modern Olympics were held, some people in the United States decided to have a marathon in this country. The very next year, in 1897, the first Boston Marathon was run. It has been held every year since then. The first winner was John J. McDermott. He ran 26 miles and 385 feet in 2 hours, 55 minutes, 10 seconds.

Read the newspaper or listen to radio and television programs for news about this year's marathon.

How many people entered? _____

How many people finished? _____

The male winner was _____

His time was _____

The female winner was _____

Her time was _____

Are these times faster or slower than Mr. McDermott's? _____

Look in an encyclopedia to find out why a marathon race is 26 miles, 385 feet in length.

April 20

Name_____

Lefty Awareness Week

All left-handed persons! This is your week! Being left-handed is not abnormal, but it can be difficult—most other people don't realize this. Many tools and activities are planned for right-handed persons—scissors, knitting, archery, even handwriting. But as intelligent people, you do your best and become successful. Hurray for left-handed persons!

Work in pairs for this project. Place the hand you use most on a piece of rather heavy white paper and have your partner trace around it. Cut it out and mount it on a sheet of colored paper. Cut slits on the solid line of each corner as shown here. Lay a ruler along each side touching the ends of the slits, and fold the edges of the paper up. Add tape at the inside of the corners to make a frame. Take your hand home to stick on the refrigerator door. Tell your family you are giving them a helping hand. Then carry through by offering your help with the dinner dishes.

April 21 Name_____

Rod Fishing Record

Do you like to go fishing? Maybe you would like to have been Alfred Dean in 1959. He cast his line off the shore of South Australia and got a nibble. When he finally landed his catch, he had a white man-eating shark. His line was supposed to be only strong enough for 130 pounds, but the shark weighed 2,664 pounds and was 16 feet, 10 inches long.

Catch your own white shark. Solve the problems in the puzzle below. Color blue any section that has an answer that is an even number. Leave white the sections whose answers are odd numbers. If correct, you will soon see a shark heading toward your line!

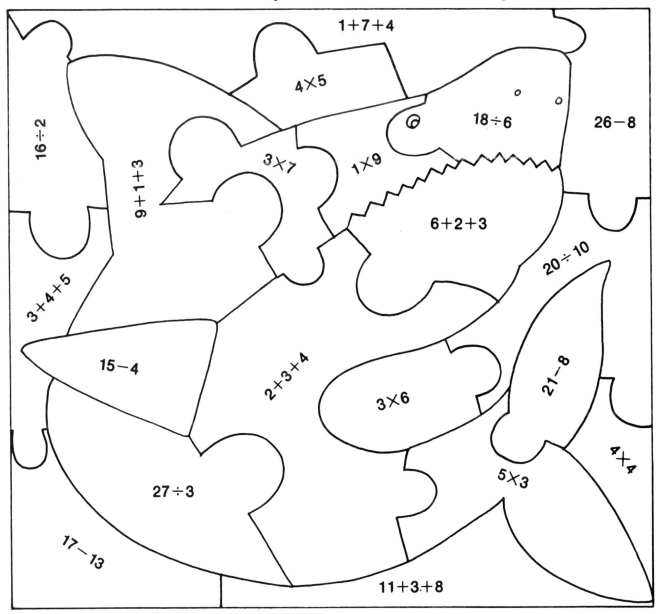

247

April 22   Name_____

Sniff-the-Breeze Day

Summer comes early in Egypt. On this day Egyptians believe "there is nothing like a few breaths of departing spring air to keep away the hot summer's mid-afternoon drowsiness." They are right. Taking deep breaths of fresh air will put more oxygen in your lungs and keep you wide awake.

Do you sometimes get sleepy when you should be reading or doing math? Try these simple exercises right at your desk. They may help to wake you up.
1. Sit up straight. Inhale as you count from 1 to 20, then exhale for the same number of counts. Do this four times.
2. Sit at your desk with feet flat on the floor. Press them as hard against the floor as you can while you count to 10. Relax, then do it again.
3. Sit at your desk with hands at sides. Press palms of your hands hard against the seat of your chair while you count to 10. Relax, then do it again.

April 23

Name _____

Keep America Beautiful

This week reminds communities to clean up, spruce up, and make their areas a better place to live in. Many communities have clean-up campaigns for picking up tree limbs, trash, and other rubbish in the neighborhood.

Keep this city block beautiful. Walk around it and pick up every fourth letter (starting with G). After four trips around, you will have picked up 10 pieces of trash and it will be a beautiful place.

April 24

Name _____

Professional Secretaries' Week

This is the week when we honor those people who work as secretaries. A good secretary must be able to type well, to file letters correctly, to use the telephone politely, and to meet and work with other people. He or she must be courteous, careful, accurate, skilled in using business machines, intelligent, and use good common sense.

Make a card to give to your school secretary. Fold a sheet of 9" x 12" paper in half crosswise, then crosswise again. Put a large "thank you" on the outside. On the inside write three reasons why the school secretary is a good person for your school.

250

April 25

Name _____

First Car License

On April 25, 1901, New York State passed the first automobile license law. Owners had to give their names, addresses, and a description of their automobiles. The law said that each license plate would contain the owner's initials and must be over three inches high. Today every state and province has a license law.

Some license plates have special slogans or drawings to describe a state or province. Draw the license plate of your state or province. If you cannot remember exactly what it is like, look out the window at a car parked nearby.

Do you think your state's plate is interesting? Would you like to have it changed? On another sheet of paper, draw your own idea of what your state's plate should look like.

April 26   Name_____

John James Audubon Born

John James Audubon, born in 1785, was one of the first persons to study and paint birds of North America. His drawings showed birds nesting, feeding, fighting, flying, feeding their young, and so on. He took as much care in drawing the trees and limbs on which birds roosted as he did the birds themselves. The first pictures published were black and white drawings that Audubon colored with watercolors.

Experiment with colors. Use pastel crayons or colored chalk to color this picture. Shade the colors so the feathers seem to blend into one another. This bird is a blue jay. You can use a bird book as a guide for coloring, or create a fanciful bird, blending and shading many colors.

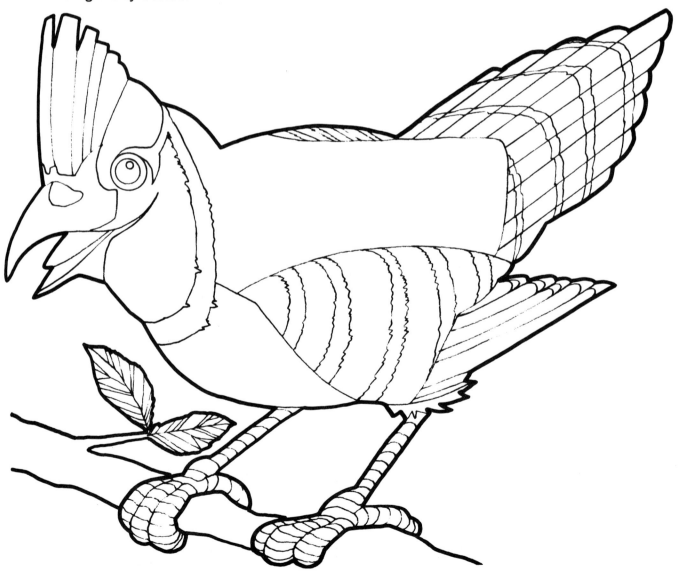

April 27

Name_____

A New Town

In 1906 the United States Steel Corporation began building a new steel plant. It was halfway between the iron ore mines and the fields of coal that would be needed to run the smelting furnaces. The people who would work in this plant needed homes nearby, so the company had to build a town. And it did. That town is now the city of Gary, Indiana.

If you are building a city, what are some of the things you must provide? Here is the start of a list of all the services necessary for life in a community. Add to it. Keep the list handy. As you think of other things, add them.

schools
paved streets
water lines

_____

_____

_____

_____

_____

_____

April 28

Name_____

Columbus' Ships Return

Persons who had not read the newspapers must have rubbed their eyes in amazement in New York City in 1893. Moving down the harbor were exact replicas of Columbus' ships, the *Nina*, *Pinta*, and the *Santa Maria*. They were followed by 35 warships from 10 nations. All had come to honor the 400th anniversary of Columbus' discovery of America.

Today many nations own a large sailing vessel that they use for training cadets. The U.S. training ship is the *Eagle*. These tall ships often gather to form a naval parade, just as the ships did in 1893. There was a parade for the U.S. Bicentennial in 1976 and Eastern Canada celebrations in 1984.

Here are the names of some of the sailing ships and the countries that own them. But the country names are mixed up. Unscramble the countries so you'll know who owns these interesting ships.

Amerigo Vespucci	YTIAL _____
Esmeralda	ELHCI _____
Danmark	MEDKRAN _____
Kruzenshtern	SARIUS _____
Christian Radich	RYANOW _____
Nippon Maru	PAANJ _____
Gorch Fock	EMYGRAN _____
Libertad	TIANNERAG _____

254

Patent for Zipper

In 1913 Gideon Sundback obtained a patent for a kind of fastener that used a slide to close an opening. Nine years later, the B. F. Goodrich Company began to make rubber-coated boots that had these slide fasteners. The boots were called "zippers" because of the sound their fasteners made as they opened and closed. Soon people forgot that zipper meant the boots and began to call all slide fasteners zippers.

The Goodrich Company used *onomatopoeia* when it named its boots. Onomatopoeia is the use of words that imitate the sounds they make. See if you can fill this page with words that sound like what they mean. Here are some to get you started.

April 30

Name_____

Washington Inaugurated

On this day in 1789, George Washington became the first U.S. president. The ceremony was in New York City, the nation's first capital. It was a Thursday morning. At 9:00 A.M. services were held in New York City churches. At noon a military procession led a carriage with the president to Federal Hall. He took his oath of office on a balcony over a street as thousands of people watched. Washington's inauguration for the second term was held on March 4, and that date was used for the inauguration every year until 1937. By then the 20th Amendment had been passed, which said that a president's term shall end at noon on January 20. Since then inaugurations have been held at noon on that day.

Think about these questions:

1. The 20th Amendment shortened the time between when a person was elected and when he or she took office. Is this a good idea? _____

Why? _____

_____

_____

2. A lame duck is someone weak or helpless. This amendment is called the lame duck amendment. Can you tell why? _____

_____

_____

_____

May 1

Law Day

For hundreds of years, May 1 has been a day of celebrations. Some people celebrate it as a spring festival, with flowers and dances. Some countries observe it as a worker's holiday. In the United States we honor it as Law Day. This is a day to think about our laws—to respect and support them, and to understand their importance in the life of every citizen.

Think about what a country would be like with no laws. Write a story telling what happened on "The Day There Were No Traffic Laws."

May 2 Name _____

Older Americans Month

Each year the president sets aside May as Older Americans Month. It is a time when we stop to think about our older citizens and the valuable contributions they have made to our country.

How many older people do you know? List the names of three of them here. After each name, tell something you can do for that person this month. If the person lives nearby, you might run errands for him or her or pay a visit each week. A person living far away might enjoy a card or letter. Put a star by the activity you're going to do right away, then make plans to do it.

1. _____

_____

_____

2. _____

_____

_____

3. _____

_____

_____

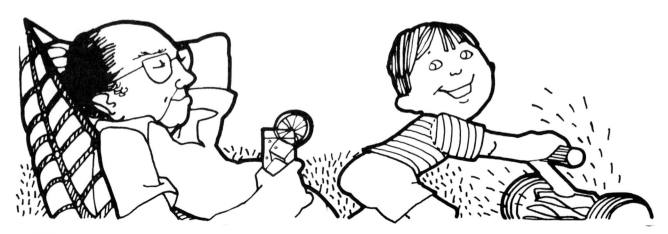

May 3

Name _____

The Columbian Exposition

In 1893 the World's Columbian Exposition opened in Chicago. The purpose was to celebrate the 400th anniversary of the discovery of America, even though it was a year late. Many new inventions and machines were on display. The exposition used more electricity than the whole city of Chicago at that time. Its Palace of Fine Arts building is now Chicago's Museum of Science and Industry. G.W. Gale Ferris invented a huge riding wheel especially for the fair. It was called a Ferris wheel. The wheel was 250 feet in diameter and had 36 cars. Each car could hold 60 persons, so 2,160 people could ride at one time. It was the largest Ferris wheel ever built.

Carnivals, fairs, and amusement parks have all kinds of rides. List five of your favorite ones here and tell what sort of ride each one is. Beside each ride put a number from 1 to 5 to rate how scary it is—1 for the calmest ride, 5 for the scariest.

1. _____

2. _____

3. _____

4. _____

5. _____

May 4

Name _____

Invisible Ink

On this day in 1776, Silas Deane arrived in France to purchase military supplies for the colonies. He was afraid he might be captured by the English, so his instructions were written in invisible ink. Two chemicals were used, one to write the message, the other to read the message.

You can make and use invisible ink. Write a simple message on rather thin paper, using a fine brush dipped in milk, lemon juice, or a thin syrup of sugar and water. Let it dry. To decode the message, you just heat the paper. Have an adult friend hold it over a light bulb until the milk, juice, or syrup turns brown.

May 5

Name _____

National Physical Fitness and Sports Month

This is a month to think about summer and summer sports. What are your favorite ones—softball, swimming, hiking, camping, water skiing? If you don't have one, begin to learn one. Make this a summer to get really fit.

Play this game with your friends. It is called "In The Ditch" and is like "Simon Says" but takes more energy. Lay two parallel strings of yarn about 18 inches apart along the floor. One side of the yarn is the bank, the other side is the ditch. Choose a leader. The rest of the players space themselves along the yarn that's on the bank side. The leader orders players to jump from side to side by calling out their names and then "In the ditch" or "On the bank." He or she tries to trick players by calling the orders quickly and then by repeating the same direction. (If the leader calls out "Terry, in the ditch," and Terry is already in the ditch, he remains standing there.) If a person jumps the wrong way, he or she drops out. The winner is the last person left and becomes the new leader for the next game.

May 6   Name _____

First Postage Stamp

Today is the birthday of the first adhesive postage stamp, issued in 1840. It was a one-penny stamp called the Penny Black of Great Britain. By 1860 almost every country had adopted stamps as a way to pay a letter's postage before it was delivered. Before that, the person receiving the letter had to pay the postage.

Every year post office departments around the world publish many new stamps. Sometimes a stamp will celebrate the anniversary of an important event. Design a stamp to celebrate the closing of school for the summer. What kind of symbol might you use? What denomination will it be—1¢, 20¢, 35¢? Use scrap paper for your first sketches, then put your stamp design here.

May 7   Name_____

Happy Birthday, Francis Beaufort

This man, born in 1774, became an admiral in the British navy. In 1805 he used numbers to estimate or show wind speeds. His system is called the Beaufort Wind Scale. Here it is.

1	Light air	Weather vanes inactive; smoke drifts with the air
2	Light breeze	Weather vanes active; leaves rustle
3	Gentle breeze	Leaves and small twigs move
4	Moderate breeze	Dust and loose paper blow about
5	Fresh breeze	Small trees sway
6	Strong breeze	Large branches sway; umbrellas are hard to use
7	Moderate gale	Whole trees sway; it's hard to walk against the wind
8	Fresh gale	Walking against the wind is very difficult
9	Strong gale	Shingles blow off roof
10	Whole gale	Trees are uprooted
11	Storm	Widespread damage
12	Hurricane	Violent destruction

Watch the winds today. Write down the number you think the strongest wind was, according to this scale. In general was this a calm or a windy day?

Take this scale home to keep. You can impress your family by telling them if it is a 2-, a 4-, or a 7-wind day.

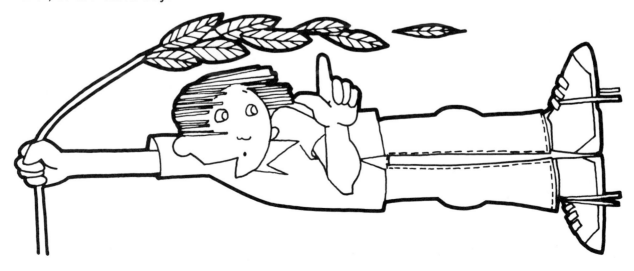

Coke Is It!

Customers at Jacob's Pharmacy in Atlanta, Georgia, had a real treat on this day in 1886. For the first time ever, people could buy a soft drink called Coca-Cola. Soft drinks are often called pop because the first bottle caps made a loud noise when they came off. In some places a soft drink is called soda. Almost all soft drinks contain flavorings, sugar, and something called soda water. But soda water has no soda. It is water that carbon dioxide gas has been put into. As the gas escapes, the water bubbles. Many soft drinks have fruit flavorings as well—lemon, lime, orange, strawberry, raspberry, cherry. Cola drinks are flavored by the kola nut, a seed of an evergreen tree that grows in tropic areas.

You can make a kind of soft drink. It will not taste like the ones you buy, but it will have carbon dioxide bubbles. Fill a glass 2/3 full of fruit juice or a fruit drink. If it is not sweet, add a little sugar. Then add 1/2 teaspoon cream of tartar and 1/4 teaspoon baking soda. Stir a few seconds until it is bubbly. Taste it. You may not want to drink all of it, but you can see and taste the carbon dioxide. If your mother will let you experiment, you may be able to find a combination of flavors that you rather like.

May 9   Name_____

A Bank for Eyes

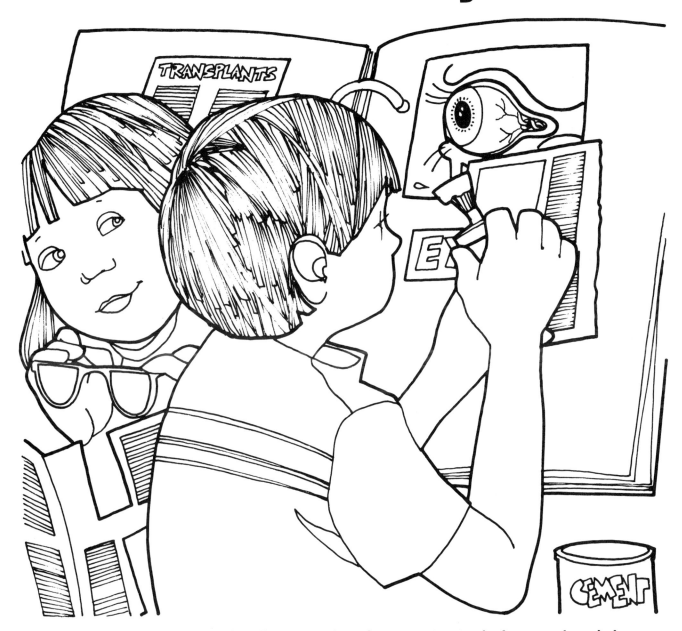

On this day in 1944, the first eye bank was started. An eye bank is a place that stores eye parts and then sends them to persons who need them. Eye corneas were among the first organs to be transplanted from one person's body to another's. Today transplants are being made of kidneys, livers, even hearts and lungs, as well as eye corneas.

Start a class collection of newspaper and magazine clippings about people who have recently had some kind of organ transplant. Perhaps someone in your city has had this operation. Watch for any news of his or her recovery.

May 10   Name _____

First Mother's Day

For many years Anna Jarvis had wanted a special day to honor mothers. Finally, because of her work, churches in Philadelphia, Pennsylvania, and in Grafton, West Virginia, held Mother's Day celebrations on May 10, 1908. The idea grew, and in 1914 President Wilson announced the second Sunday in May would be a national day to honor mothers.

Make a medal for Mother. Check the school scrap box for a plastic top from a coffee can or other container. Decorate the edges by pasting on yarn scraps. In the center, with felt pens, write a slogan or some words of love. Punch a small hole and add yarn to hang around Mother's neck.

May 11

Name_____

Native American Day

The second Saturday in May is often celebrated as a tribute to this country's first people. We have much to thank the early Indians for. They introduced new settlers to squash, corn, and pecans. They taught them ways to fertilize the land and how to cure hides. Many of the words in our language come from one of the Indian languages. A few of these words are *moose, skunk, toboggan, caribou, raccoon,* and *succotash.* The game of lacrosse is based on a game played by the Indians of northeast America.

Twenty of our states have Indian names. Here are nine of them. Can you draw a line from each state in the left-hand column to its original Indian name on the right?

Wyoming	arizonac (the place of the small spring)
Mississippi	kentake (meadow land)
Ohio	mica gama (big water)
Michigan	quinnitukgut (at the long tidal river)
Nebraska	mici sibi (big river)
Kentucky	oheo (beautiful water)
Connecticut	mache-weaming (at the big flats)
Arizona	aijuba (the sleepy one)
Iowa	ni-bthaska (river in the flatness)

Limerick Day

Today is Limerick Day, in honor of a man who made this verse popular. Edward Lear, an English writer born in 1812, is remembered for his many limericks and for his humorous poems for children. A limerick has five lines. Lines 1, 2, and 5 rhyme; lines 3 and 4 rhyme. Usually the first line begins, "There was a . . ." This is one of Lear's limericks.

> There was an old man with a beard,
> Who said, "It is just as I feared—
> Two owls and a hen
> Four larks and a wren
> Have all built their nests in my beard."

Write your own limerick. The three longest lines have eight syllables, the two shorter ones have five syllables.

There was a _____

_____

_____

_____

_____

Ask at the library for some books that contain Lear's limericks and other poems.

May 13

Name _____

Stevie Wonder's Birthday

Today is Stevie Wonder's birthday. Born in 1950, this blind musician recorded his first song, "Fingertips," when he was only 12 years old. Stevie sings, plays the piano, and composes.

One of his recent hits is called "Happy Birthday." He wrote it to honor Martin Luther King, Jr. and to urge our government to make King's birthday a national holiday.

Stevie feels there ought to be a world party for peace each year on King's birthday. Suppose you were in charge of this party.

Where would be a good place to hold the party? _____

_____

What get-acquainted game would you plan for people who do not speak the same language? _____

_____

What entertainment would show the partygoers about peace? _____

_____

What food would you serve? _____

_____

What would be a good song for everyone to sing as they start home after the party?

_____

May 14

Name_____

Permanent English Settlement

On May 14, 1607, about 100 men from three ships landed on the shores of Virginia and started a settlement. They called it Jamestown for King James I of England. This was the first permanent English settlement in America.

How is your math? Use it to find out how many years have passed between the beginning of the Jamestown colony in 1607 and:

1. The arrival of the Pilgrims in 1620. _____

2. The birth of George Washington in 1732. _____

3. The writing of the Declaration of Independence in 1776. _____

4. The birth of Abraham Lincoln in 1809. _____

5. The discovery of gold in California in 1848. _____

6. The end of the Civil War in 1865. _____

7. The end of World War II in 1945. _____

8. The forming of Alaska and Hawaii as states in 1959. _____

9. The year when you were born. _____

10. The year this is. _____

May 15

Name _____

Wizard's Father Has Birthday

Lyman Frank Baum was a newspaperman, born in 1856, who became a children's book writer. Baum's office had file cabinets with the drawers marked for alphabetical filing. One drawer was labeled O-Z. Baum used these two letters as the name of a fantasy land, Oz, where all sorts of things happened. Altogether he wrote 14 books about the land of Oz, but the most famous one is *The Wonderful Wizard of Oz.*

One of the journeys through Oz follows a yellow brick road. Follow your own brick road to the castle where the Wizard lives. Think of names of people and animals in your reading book and in other books you have read. Write one of these names in each brick (the Wizard has already started the trip for you), until you get to the castle at the end.

May 16

Name_____

The Pied Piper Plays

Each Sunday from May to September, visitors in the town of Hameln, Germany can see a play about an old legend. The legend says that hundreds of years ago, Hameln had many rats. Then someone came to town and promised to get rid of them for a fee. The mayor agreed but when the rats were gone, he refused to pay. The man became so angry, he played a strange melody on his pipe and all the village children followed him to a cave in the hill. They were never seen again. The legend is based on one fact—many children did leave the town rather suddenly. Today people think the piper was a person looking for young people to settle in another part of Germany.

Pretend that the father in a family next door got a new job in another part of the country. The family moved very quickly during the school's spring vacation. When school opened on Monday morning, the house was empty and the family was gone. Create your own legend to explain to others why the family seemed to have disappeared so mysteriously.

_____

_____

_____

_____

_____

_____

_____

_____

May 17

Name _____

Saved by the Seagulls

In Temple Square in Salt Lake City, Utah, there is a tall statue showing two seagulls hovering over a globe. It is dedicated to the seagulls who live around Great Salt Lake. In 1848 the new settlers had irrigated their land and their crops were growing well. Suddenly huge swarms of grasshoppers appeared and began to eat the crops. But the seagulls also appeared and ate the grasshoppers before the crops were ruined.

Do you know what a grasshopper looks like? Counting by 3s, connect the numbered dots from 3 to 66. When finished you'll have a picture of this pest.

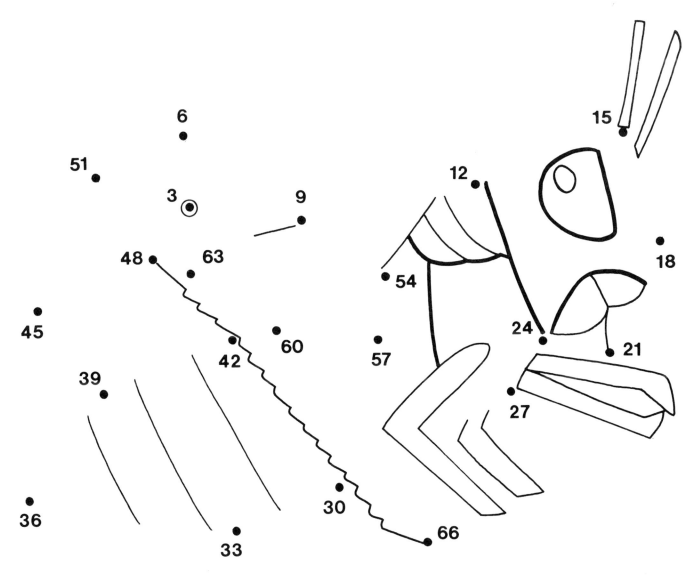

273

May 18

Name_____

Mount St. Helens Erupts

On this day in 1980, Mount St. Helens blew up. A huge explosion sent steam and ashes more than 11 miles into the sky where the wind blew it over parts of three states. More explosions took off the top and part of one side of the mountain. Dirt and stones slid down its sides, filling a lake and streams and turning huge trees into toothpicks.

You can make a simple model of a volcano. Find a box about two feet square and cut the sides down so they are about three inches high. Cut a hole in the middle of the box's bottom the same size as a paper towel tube. Now take a paper towel tube and tape it upright over the hole. Place the box on wooden blocks and put the end of a bicycle pump into the bottom of the tube, from underneath the box. Tape it in place and tape shut the rest of the tube's bottom. Make a mountain by piling sand, dirt, or crushed newspapers and papier mache around the tube. Fill the tube with dry oatmeal, or any light material. Briskly pump the bicycle pump and watch the oatmeal blow out of the top of the mountain. It will give the same effect as the steam and ash that blew out of Mount St. Helens.

May 19   Name_____

Frog-Jumping Jubilee

One of Mark Twain's best stories is about a frog jumping contest. The owner of a frog, called Dan'l Webster, insisted no other frog could jump farther than his, but an opponent fed the frog buckshot so it was too heavy to jump. On this day in 1928, the first Frog Jumping Jubilee was held at Angels Camp, California, in honor of Twain's story. Fifty-one frogs were entered in the contest. The winner was "The Pride of San Joaquin," who jumped three feet, four inches. The jubilee has been held every year since.

Make a frog puppet, using a plastic hamburger container from a fast food store. Paint it green. Add eyes and a red tongue. Use your puppet to tell about the contest as if you were the winning frog.

May 20

Name _____

First Speeding Arrest

In 1899 Jacob German, who was a taxi driver for the Electric Vehicle Company, was arrested. He was driving at a "breakneck speed" of 12 miles per hour on Lexington Avenue in New York City. He was booked and jailed by a bicycle roundsman, a police patrolman who covered his rounds by bicycle.

Highway signs tell speed limits and other driving rules. Here are some of the most common signs. Beside each one, tell what the sign asks drivers to do.

May 21   Name _____

Mystery Ride

The Missouri Pacific Railroad wanted more people to ride its trains. It needed this money to keep the trains running. So on this Saturday in 1932, it started offering people an unusual kind of train trip—a "mystery excursion" ride. People paid for a ticket and got on board at St. Louis, but they didn't know where they would end up! Many people enjoyed this weekend surprise.

Write a short story about a "mystery excursion" that you took. How did you go—by ship, plane, train, bus, rocket? Where did you end up—the next town, city, country, planet? What exciting things did you do and find there?

May 22

Name _____

National Maritime Day

National Maritime Day is a day to honor the steamship *Savannah*. On May 22, 1819, it left Savannah, Georgia, for Liverpool, England. This wooden ship had sails as well as a steam engine. Steam power was used on this ship for only 80 to 100 hours, but the *Savannah* is still known as the first steamship to cross the Atlantic Ocean. People called it a steam coffin and were afraid of it; although it had 32 staterooms, no passengers dared to make the trip.

National Maritime Day is a good time to think about boat safety, especially the small boats used on lakes and rivers. Make up 2 short verses on good and bad boat habits. This verse may give you some ideas.
   There once was a man by the name of Drake,
   Stood up in a boat and fell in the lake.

1. _____

_____

2. _____

_____

May 23

Name _____

International Pickle Week

This is a week to honor the "world's most humorous vegetable." Most pickles are made by preserving cucumbers with vinegar, salt, and spices. Ask your mother to make sure she serves pickles at a meal sometime during the week.

Start a collection of pickle jokes and riddles. You'll find them in riddle books, but you can also make up your own. Here are a few to get you started.

What is green and flies?
Superpickle.

If you cross a cat and a pickle, what do you have?
A picklepuss.

What is green and dangerous?
A thundering herd of pickles.

What is green and pecks on trees?
Woody Woodpickle.

What is green and goes "click, click, click?"
A ball-point pickle.

May 24

Name _____

Victoria Day

The citizens of Canada celebrate Victoria Day in honor of the birthday of Queen Victoria, who was born May 24, 1819. It is also a day to honor the present-day king or queen of the British Commonwealth of Nations. Victoria was queen of the British Empire for 63 years, longer than any other British monarch. While she was queen, the colonies of British North America were united into the Dominion of Canada. The colonies in Australia were also united and became the Commonwealth of Australia.

Many places in countries that were part of the British Empire during Queen Victoria's life were named after her. Use an atlas to find a city, lake, waterfall, and desert named for her. Tell the country it is in today.

Country

city _____ _____

lake _____ _____

waterfall _____ _____

desert _____ _____

Find four more Victorias and tell what they are, and where they are located.

Name	What It Is	Country
_____	_____	_____
_____	_____	_____
_____	_____	_____
_____	_____	_____

May 25 Name_____

A Time Capsule

On this day in 1940, students at Oglethorpe University in Atlanta, Georgia, packed a time capsule. They put thousands of small objects used in daily life, motion pictures, and microfilms into a large container which was then sealed. The capsule was buried under one of the college buildings and is not to be opened until the year 8113. Libraries, universities, and temples around the world have information about the capsule and where it is buried.

Create your own time capsule. Put these things in a small box—lists of favorite games, toys, and books; a drawing of your family or classmates; a paragraph about your favorite subject. Seal the box and mark it to be opened in one year. Put the box away in your closet. When you open it next year, you'll have fun examining all the things in the box.

May 26

Name_____

Happy Birthday, Sally Ride

Dr. Sally Ride, born today in 1951, is one of seven women in the U.S. astronaut corps. Her flight on space shuttle *Challenger* made her the first U.S. woman in space. *Challenger* was launched June 18, 1983, and landed on June 24. It was a near-perfect mission.

Did you know that you would be taller in space than you are here on earth? When you don't have gravity to hold you down, your joints and bones spread apart. Try this astronaut experiment. Tonight, just before you go to bed, have someone measure your height. Then tomorrow morning before you come to school, have that person measure you again. You may be 1/4 inch taller in the morning! That's because you have been lying down and at rest for a long time, and gravity hasn't been pulling you down. Try measuring younger brothers and sisters. The differences in their heights may be even greater, perhaps almost a half inch.

Golden Gate Bridge

In 1937 the Golden Gate Bridge was opened. This is one of the largest and most beautiful suspension bridges in the world. It is 8,981 feet long and connects northern California and the San Francisco peninsula. It stretches across the entrance to San Francisco Bay. Any ship coming to San Francisco must pass under this bridge. It's called a suspension bridge because it is suspended from steel cables that are fastened to high towers on each bank of the bay.

Here are sketches of some different kinds of bridges. Draw a line from each drawing to its correct name.

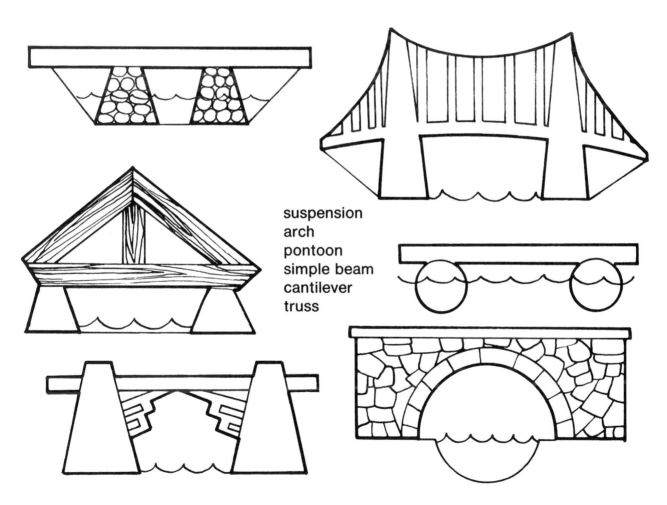

suspension
arch
pontoon
simple beam
cantilever
truss

Use a dictionary or encyclopedia to find the meaning of one of these words. Write its meaning here.

May 28

Name _____

No Fishing!

On this day in 1734, New York City passed a law to protect fish in the nearby fresh-water ponds. Fishing could only be done with a rod, hook, and line. It was illegal to use nets of any kind, machines, or any other contraptions.

Here are some of this country's most common fresh-water fish. Unscramble their names. Then underline the names of any fish that live in your part of the country. If you go fishing, put an X beside any kinds of fish you have caught.

tommalshul sasb _____

tomergahul sasb _____

helancn ftachsi _____

elub lilg _____

woylle creph _____

broniwa rutto _____

hooc mnalos _____

kleenuumslg _____

therronn keip _____

dlabuhle _____

May 29

Name _____

Conquerors of Mount Everest

On this day in 1953, Sir Edmund Hillary and Tenzing Norgay reached the top of Mount Everest. They were the first men ever to climb this mountain. Mount Everest is in the Himalaya Mountains in Asia and is the highest peak in the world.

Can you climb this Mount Everest? When people climb a steep and dangerous mountain, they usually set up camps along the way. Start at the bottom, and find your way to Camp 1, then to Camp 2, and finally to the top.

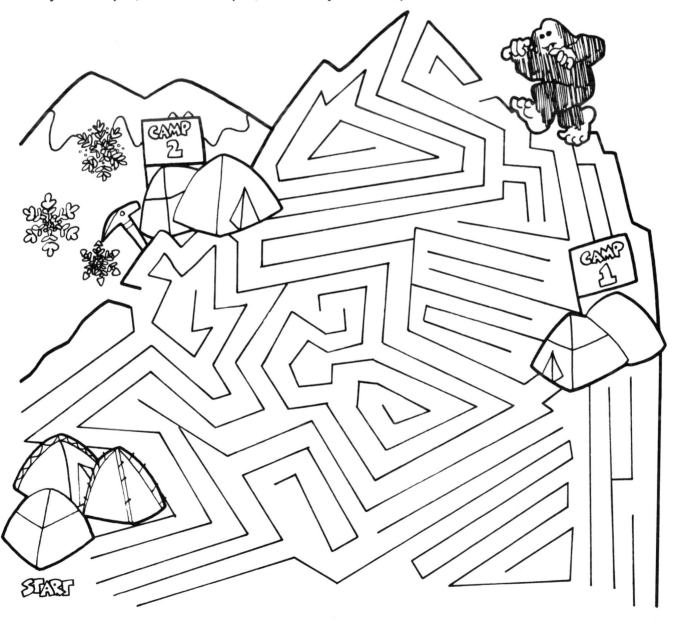

May 30   Name_____

Memorial Day

Memorial Day began as a day when people decorated the graves of soldiers who had died in the Civil War. It was called Decoration Day and was observed on May 30. Today we spend it remembering veterans of all wars, and we observe it on the last Monday in May.

After World War I, veterans began to sell red silk poppies at this time of year. The money was used to buy medicine and other supplies for disabled veterans. The poppy had become a symbol of hope to them, because it grew and blossomed on fields in Europe that had been destroyed by gunfire.

Many people hang plates on their walls as a souvenir of a place or an event. Design a paper plate as a souvenir of Memorial Day. Use the red poppy as a part of your design.

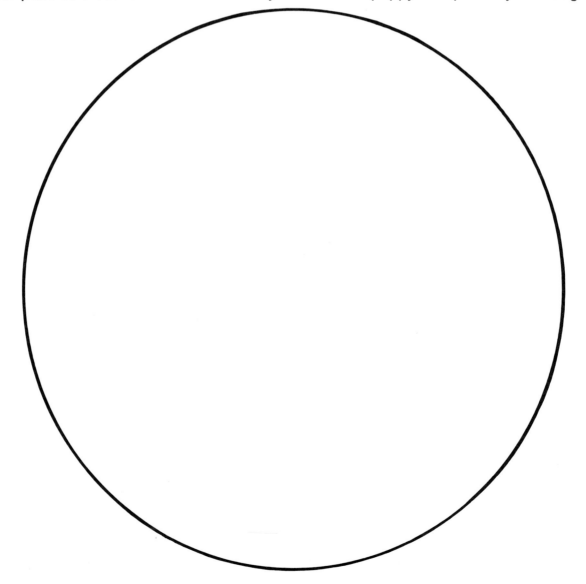

May 31 Name_____

Copyright Law Passed

President George Washington signed the first copyright law on May 31, 1790. This is a law that says printed materials belong to their authors and cannot be copied. Short stories, poems, books, magazines, music, maps, charts, and other materials can be copyrighted so no one can copy them without permission. When something is copyrighted, it contains a notice that tells the name of the person or company that owns it and the year it was copyrighted. Sometimes a book will list several years to show that changes were made in the book in those years and new copyrights were given.

Find the copyright notices in three books. It is usually on page 2, on the back of the page with the title on it. Write them here.

1. _____
   _____

2. _____
   _____

3. _____
   _____

Look for a copyright notice in a magazine. You'll probably find it somewhere on the first five pages. Write it here.

_____
_____

Find a notice on a map, chart, piece of music, or poster. Write it here.

_____
_____

June 1

Name _____

Don't Give Up the Ship!

It was June 1, 1813, and there was a battle at sea. Captain James Lawrence had been wounded, but he still urged his ship's crew to keep on fighting. "Don't give up the ship!" he gasped. His ship was finally captured, but Lawrence's plea became a navy slogan. The words were put on a flag and flown during another naval battle later that year. Today people still use Lawrence's words to urge someone to keep trying when he or she is faced with a tough problem.

Cut out these letters and arrange them on a sheet of blue paper. Take it home to hang in your room. When you think your chores at home are too many or that your math problems are too hard, just remember Lawrence's words.

June 2 Name _____

First Night Baseball Game

Would you believe that people have been watching night baseball games for over 100 years? The very first night game was played in Fort Wayne, Indiana, on June 2, 1883. Two thousand people watched as the Quincey professionals played the M.E. College team in a game seven innings long. Quincey won, 19 to 11.

Today many sports and entertainment activities, like basketball and rock music concerts, take place at night. List as many as you can think of. Put an X beside any that take place in your city. Underline the ones you would like to attend.

June 3

Name _____

Charles Drew Born

We can thank this man, born in 1904, for the blood banks we have today. Dr. Drew, a black physician, was the first director of the Red Cross program to collect blood for the U.S. armed forces. He convinced other physicians to just use the plasma part of blood (liquid part) when collecting and giving blood, because it can be stored for long periods of time and be given to persons of any blood type. This is important in times of war or when some disaster such as an earthquake hits a city. Blood plasma saved millions of lives in World War II. Today about 10 million pints of blood are collected every year. Most of the people giving blood are volunteers and are not paid for their blood. Healthy persons can give a pint of blood several times a year. Their bodies will restore the amount lost in a few weeks. Giving blood is one way people can help those who are ill or injured.

Use the underlined words above to complete the puzzle below.

Hurrah for Roquefort Cheese!

The story says that a monk accidentally made Roquefort cheese in 1070. Here's how. One day he left his lunch in a cave near Roquefort, France, and didn't go back to get it. A few days later, June 4 to be exact, he went back to the cave. The cheese in his lunch, made from sheep's milk, had a very new flavor. Today, true Roquefort cheese is still made from sheep's milk and is cured in the caves near Roquefort, France. It is a strong-tasting cheese with streaks of blue in it—these streaks are mold. Most molds make food uneatable but the blue streaks in Roquefort are a special kind of mold that gives the cheese its flavor.

There are more than 400 kinds of cheese. They are made of the milk from many kinds of animals, from cows to yaks to camels to zebras. Here are the names of some of the most common kinds of cheese. Use them to complete this crossword puzzle.

BRIE   BLUE   COTTAGE   CREAM   CHEDDAR   EDAM
MONTEREY JACK   MUNSTER   PARMESAN   ROQUEFORT

June 5

Name _____

First Hot-Air Balloon Flight

Two brothers, Joseph and Jacques Montgolfier made history on this day in 1783 in France. A balloon they had made and filled with hot air rose about 1,500 feet into the air. It was carried by the wind for over a mile before it landed 10 minutes later. Three months later they launched another balloon; this one was carrying a duck, rooster, and sheep as passengers. It flew for 8 minutes, and all the animals returned safely. Later that same year, there was another hot-air balloon flight, this time with two men as passengers. They were in the air for 25 minutes and traveled 6 miles.

Pretend you are a passenger in a hot-air balloon, looking down on the countryside as you float along. Draw a picture of your school as it looks from your balloon.

June 6

Name _____

First Drive-In Movie

On this day in 1933, the first drive-in movie theater opened, in Camden, New Jersey. People could sit in their cars and watch two shows a night on a screen that was 40 by 50 feet. The parking places were on a slant so viewers could see the screen more easily.

Have you ever been to a drive-in movie? They're fun! You can wear old clothes, take all kinds of snacks, and be able to talk and wiggle without disturbing others. Sometimes young boys and girls wear pajamas, so they are all ready for bed when they get home again.

The word "drive-in" has a long vowel sound and a short vowel sound. Look at the words below. Color green all the areas that have short-vowel words. Color pink the areas that have long-vowel words. When done correctly, you will find the shape of a favorite movie cartoon character.

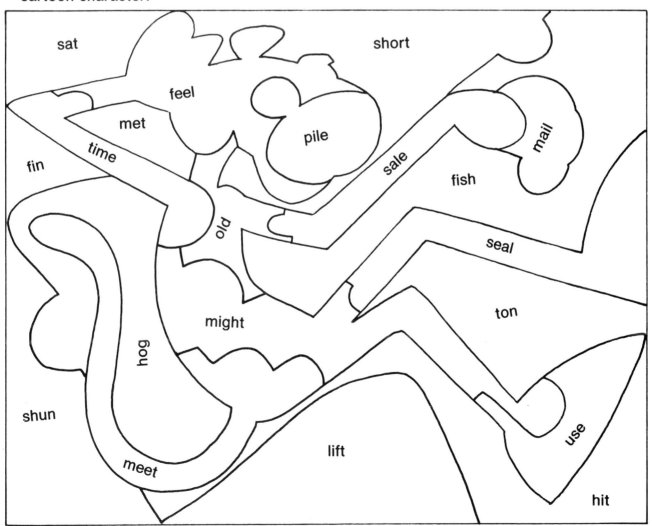

June 7   Name_____

Two Poets Born

Today is the birthday of two important black poets. Gwendolyn Brooks was born in 1917, Nikki Giovanni in 1943. Ms. Brooks grew up in a part of Chicago nicknamed Bronzeville. One of her books of poems, called *Bronzeville Boys and Girls*, contains poems about the experiences and thoughts of black boys and girls living in the city. Andre, for example, dreamed he had to choose a father and mother. He wondered what he should do, then finally chose the parents he had. There is a poem about "Eldora Who Is Rich," "John Who Is Poor," "Cynthia in the Snow," and "Michael Is Afraid of the Storm." Ms. Giovanni also writes about the lives of blacks. Her poems often contain interesting rhythms.

Write a four-line poem about a boy or girl you know and something special about him or her. Use a title like "Bill Who Plays Baseball," "Mary Who Likes to Cook," or "Tony is Everyone's Friend."

_____

_____

_____

_____

Ask at the library for books that have poems by Ms. Brooks and Ms. Giovanni.

June 8

Name _____

Frank Lloyd Wright Born

Born in 1869, Frank Lloyd Wright was a well-known architect. An architect is a person who designs buildings and then supervises their construction. When architects design a building, they must first know what it will be used for and how much space will be needed. Then they plan the size and arrangement of rooms in the building. Mr. Wright thought a building and its surroundings should go together. Many of the homes he designed seem to almost grow out of the ground.

Become an architect and plan a home you'd like to live in. First decide what kind of house it would be. Would it be in the city or country? On a hill? Beside the shore of a lake, river, or sea? How many floors would it have? What kind of material would it be made of? Now draw a picture of the outside of your dream house.

June 9

Name_____

Donald Duck Born

On this day in 1934, Donald Duck first appeared on the movie screen. He was one of the characters in a Disney cartoon called "The Wise Little Hen." Donald has three nephews, Huey, Dewey, and Louie, who often play tricks on him. Once in a while his Uncle Scrooge also appears with him.

Help Huey, Dewey, and Louie make a birthday cake for Uncle Donald. Decorate this cake for a party with Donald's friends. Plan the decorations on scrap paper, then draw them on the cake top. Color them with crayons or colored pencils.

June 10

Name_____

First Forest Fire Watcher

On this day in 1905, William Hilton began an important new job. He became the first person in the United States to watch for forest fires. A lumber company in Maine had built a log cabin with a flat roof on Squaw Mountain. Mr. Hilton stood on the roof and looked around for any sign of a forest fire. Today forest rangers and other persons have jobs like Mr. Hilton's. Most of them work in tall lookout towers like this one.

Climb this tower. Start by writing the name of a kind of tree on the first step. On the second step write the name of a tree that begins with the last letter of the first tree's name. On the third step write a tree name that begins with the last letter of the second tree's name, and keep using this method to write a tree name on each step. Can you reach the top? Use an encyclopedia or a book about trees if you need help.

June 11   Name

Happy Birthday, Jacques Cousteau

Born in 1910 in France, Jacques Cousteau is known throughout the world for his explorations of the oceans and other bodies of water. His books, films, and television specials have taught us much about life under the seas.

Where do you think Mr. Cousteau should go for the next expedition on his ship *Calypso*? Write a letter suggesting a spot and ask if you can go with him. Tell why you think your place should be explored, and describe the kinds of things you would hope to find there. Tell him the kind of help you could give him on his trip. Could you help with chores on the ship, keep a written record of everything you do and see every day, or help the film crew set up their equipment?

Girls Play Little League

Many girls jumped for joy on this day in 1974. The Little League organization changed its rules to allow girls to play on Little League baseball teams. To be a Little League player, you must be between 8 and 12 years old. The Little League baseball diamond is smaller than a regulation field. The bats are no longer than 33 inches, and the balls weigh 5 to 5¼ ounces.

Play this ball game with a friend. Pick problems from your math book and write one beside each team member. Have your friend do the same thing. Now trade papers. You solve your friend's problems, and he or she solves yours. For every correct answer, you get one run. Compare your runs with your friend's. Who has the most runs and wins the ball game?

June 13

Name _____

A Long Speech

In 1935 Senator Huey Long from Louisiana did not want a certain law passed, so he made a speech in the Senate. He thought if he spoke long enough, the senators would go home before the law could be voted on. He talked for 15 hours and 35 minutes! This idea of talking for a long time to stop a vote is called filibustering.

All of us have ways to postpone something or keep someone from doing something we don't want them to do. What is something you might do to:

1. Keep from going to bed? _____

2. Put off doing your math? _____

3. Get out of carrying out the garbage? _____

4. Postpone cleaning your room? _____

5. Keep Mom and Dad from punishing you? _____

But remember, filibusters don't usually work, so your ideas probably won't either. It's better to do it and get it over with.

June 14

Name _____

Flag Day

This day celebrates the date, in 1777, when the 13 colonies adopted the design of the U.S. flag. The first official Flag Day celebration was held in 1877, on the 100th anniversary of the selection of the flag. Then people began to suggest that Flag Day be held every year. Now, each year the president proclaims Flag Day. Flags are displayed and many schools have special programs on this day.

Look in an encyclopedia or a flag book for pictures of some of the flags the colonies used before they adopted the present flag. Draw one that you like here and write its name and date below.

This is called a _____ flag.

It was used on this date _____ .

June 15

Name _____

Smile Power Day

This is a day to remind everyone how important smiling is. A smile makes a happier life for you and others, and a better, more pleasant world around us.

Create some happy cartoon faces. Find a sheet of paper thin enough to see through. Then use the outline below to trace a face shape, and add ears, eyes, nose, mouth, and hair. Draw as many faces as you wish, making each one different by using different features.

June 16

Name_____

National Hollerin' Contest

At this time each spring, a tiny community in North Carolina has a contest "to revive the almost lost art of hollerin' which was a means of communication in days long gone by."

The last day of school would be a good time to have your own "hollerin'" contest. Not in school of course, but out on the playground or school parking lot. Ask your teacher if your class can have one, and then make your plans. Ask the principal, the custodian, and the school secretary to be judges. Each contestant must take turns yelling the same phrase or word. Judges stand with their backs to the contestants and decide who has the loudest voice. Anyone entering the contest can wear the badge on this page. Color and cut it out, then pin it to your shirt or blouse. Add a blue ribbon to the badge of the winner.

June 17

Name _____

Exploring A Great River

In 1673 two Frenchmen named Father Jacques Marquette and Louis Joliet explored the Mississippi. They left the small French mission post of St. Ignace with their companions on May 17, in birchbark canoes. Here's the route they took. First they crossed Lake Michigan to Green Bay and paddled down the bay to the Fox River. They traveled on the Fox River as far as they could, then carried their canoes over land to what is now Portage, Wisconsin, on the Wisconsin River. Then they paddled down the Wisconsin River, reached the Mississippi River on June 17, and traveled south on the Mississippi to below the mouth of the Arkansas River. There they met Indians who said there were other white men farther south. They knew these other white men must be Spanish explorers so they went no farther. They returned to St. Ignace, going north on the Illinois River, across what is now Chicago, and up Lake Michigan.

Using a red pencil, trace on the map the route of Father Marquette and Mr. Joliet. Start at St. Ignace, travel to below the mouth of the Arkansas River, and return to St. Ignace again. The paragraph above will help you.

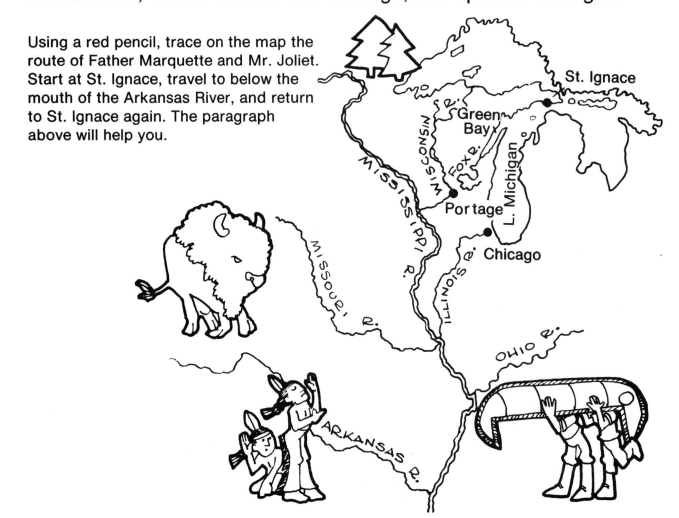

June 18

Name_____

International Picnic Day

Picnics are something that people all over the world enjoy. As soon as the weather is comfortable and there aren't too many bugs, families plan outdoor meals. Good places for a picnic are an apartment house roof or balcony, porch, patio, park, campground, or any quiet spot under a shady tree.

Bugs seem to have a way of finding picnic food. Help these ants find your picnic. Start at the anthill and find the way through the grass to the picnic lunch.

June 19

Name _____

First Father's Day

The first Father's Day was celebrated in Spokane, Washington, on this day in 1910. Today the third Sunday in June is observed as Father's Day. It is a day to do something special for your father—give a card or a gift, cook him a special meal, or perhaps wear a rose to honor him. People often wear a red rose for a living father, a white one if he has died.

Write sentences to describe what a father does or is. Start each sentence with the letters of "father."

F _____

A _____

T _____

H _____

E _____

R _____

June 20   Name _____

Ice Cream Soda Invented

On a hot, humid day in Philadelphia in 1874, an interesting demonstration took place. A company that manufactured soda fountains added ice cream to a glass of plain soda water. The first ice-cream soda! It wasn't long before someone added some flavored syrup, and soon all kinds of ice-cream sodas were being made and sold.

What is your favorite flavor of ice-cream soda? What color is it? Write a silly verse about your favorite flavor. This ridiculous rhyme may give you some ideas.
    My favorite flavor is chocolate brown.
    It cools my throat as I slurp it down.
You can do better than that! Write your verse here.

_____

_____

Tell your family what happened on this day and see if you can convince someone to celebrate by going out with you for an ice-cream soda—in your favorite flavor, of course.

Chapter 4

Still More Facts and Events

These reproducibles are for four special observances whose dates change each year, plus a page for the beginning of each season. Also in this chapter are several lists—dates the states joined the Union, dates the provinces became part of the Dominion of Canada, and birth dates of the U.S. presidents. If a reproducible for a particular day seems inappropriate for your group, you may wish to develop one from these lists. Finally, there are pages with keys to some of the puzzles and quizzes. They will save you time when pupils want to check their answers, or need help in solving a riddle.

September

Name _____

First Day of Autumn

Today is the first day of autumn. Autumn begins when the sun is directly above the equator and there is about an equal number of hours of daylight and darkness. From now on, the hours of daylight will continue to be fewer and fewer until the first day of winter.

Celebrate fall with a classroom bulletin board of leaves and leaf rubbings. Collect fallen leaves from nearby trees. Get as many different kinds as you can. Press them between hard objects, like a book and the desk, for a few hours so they will lie flat; then lay a leaf upside down on your desk. Place a paper over it. Using a crayon about the same color as the leaf, rub over the leaf to make a design or rubbing of the leaf. Cut out the rubbing and tape it and the leaf itself side by side on the bulletin board.

Can you hear any crickets chirping where you are? If you can, then you can tell the temperature with a cricket thermometer! Find a watch or clock with a second hand, then be quiet and listen to the chirps. Count the number of chirps in 14 seconds and add 40. The total you get will be the Fahrenheit temperature.

December

Name _____

First Day of Winter

Winter begins today. The sun is very low in the sky, and there is less daylight than at any other time of the year. From now until June, the hours of daylight will get longer and longer.

If you live in a part of the country where there is snow, use snowballs for this science experiment. If not, ice cubes will do just as well. Put an ice cube or a snowball in several different places—a sunny spot, shady area, tree branch, beside a brick or stone building, buried in cool dirt, and other places. Make sure the cubes or snowballs are the same size. Record the exact times they were put outside, and the exact time each one finished melting. Use this chart to record the times. When all the times are filled in, put a 1 beside the location where the cube or snowball melted first, a 2 beside the place where the snowball or cube took the next shortest time to melt, and then keep numbering the locations (3, 4, 5) in the order of how long each one took to melt.

Location	Time when I place it	Time when it finished melting
_____	_____	_____
_____	_____	_____
_____	_____	_____
_____	_____	_____
_____	_____	_____

What thing made the snowball or cube melt faster? _____

_____

What things kept it cooler? _____

_____

March   Name _____

First Day of Spring

Spring arrives today. The sun is right over the equator and there is an equal amount of daylight and darkness. The daylight hours will continue to get longer and longer until the first day of summer.

This is the season when plants begin to grow and blossom. Hurry spring along by cutting small branches, bringing them inside, and putting them in water. Use pussywillow, maple, forsythia, and other shrub branches. Watch what happens to them, and write down what you see.
Be sure you get permission before cutting!

Name of shrub _____

Date brought inside _____

What happened after one week? _____

_____

After two weeks? _____

_____

After three weeks?_____

_____

June   Name_____

First Day of Summer

Summer begins today. It is about the longest day in the year. Enjoy all this daylight today and the warm summer days to come. From now until the first day of winter, the daylight hours will be fewer and fewer.

A common spring and summer flower is the dandelion. Sometimes people used to call it shepherd's clock because the flowers open early in the day and close at night. Make these observations about the dandelions in your yard or in the park.

What time do they start to open in the morning? _____

What time do they finish opening? _____

When do they start to close in the evening? _____

How long does it take for them to close? _____

What happens to them on cloudy and rainy days? _____

_____

If there are clover, alfalfa, locust, or crown vetch plants around, watch them. Their leaves fold up at night.

November

Name _____

Election Day

The first Tuesday after the first Monday in November is election day in the United States. On that day, all eligible citizens can vote for persons to govern our nation, state, county, city, or town.

Ask your parents or read the newspapers to find out what government officers will be elected this year. Put an X beside each one below.
- ____ U.S. president and vice-president
- ____ U.S. senator
- ____ U.S. member of House of Representatives
- ____ state governor
- ____ state congressman
- ____ county executive
- ____ town supervisor
- ____ city mayor

Add any other officers that will be elected in your area.

_____ _____

_____ _____

Sometimes special laws are voted on by the people. If there is one in your community this year, write what it is about here.

_____

_____

_____

November

Name _____

Thanksgiving

When the Pilgrims decided to have a special feast of thanksgiving, the women began to bake and the men went hunting. The men returned with several wild turkeys. Ever since then, we are reminded of turkeys when we think about Thanksgiving dinner.

Create your own Thanksgiving turkey. Place your hand on this page, with fingers spread apart. Trace around it, and then turn it into a turkey. Your thumb can be the neck and head, your fingers can be the tail feathers. Draw in the legs and feet. Color the body brown, and use crayons or paste scraps of colored paper on your finger shapes to make bright tail feathers. If there are magazines you can cut up, scraps from colored pictures and advertisements are fun to use.

November/December Name _____

Hanukkah

Hanukkah is the Jewish festival of lights. During this eight-day celebration, people remember a miracle that happened long ago, when the Jewish people were fighting their enemy. After a three-year struggle, the Jews finally drove the enemy from the land. When they cleaned their temple of worship, they found only enough oil to keep the holy lamps lit for one day. But miraculously, the lamps burned for eight days.

Hanukkah is a family celebration; members exchange gifts, eat special food, read the miracle story, and light one candle each night until eight candles are burning.

Solve this Hanukkah cryptogram. Each number under the blanks below stands for a letter. The numbers that stand for the letters in "Hanukkah" are given for you. Fill in the letters you know, then try to figure out what the others might be.

```
___ ___ ___ ___   ___     ___ ___ ___ ___ ___
 1   2   6   7    2        1   2   8   8   12

H A N U K K A H   ___ ___ ___ ___ ___ ___ ___
1 2 3 4 5 5 2 1    1  10  14  18  20   2  12
```

When you have solved the puzzle, use it as the message on a card to make and send to a Jewish friend.

March/April

Name _____

Easter

A favorite custom of this Christian holiday is to decorate and exchange Easter eggs. Eggs are a symbol of the new life that begins in the spring and the new life that Christ represents. Often colored eggs are hidden, and boys and girls must hunt for them. In some countries eggs are decorated in very elaborate designs and kept from year to year.

Create your own elaborate Easter egg. Use crayons to color this entire egg shape with stripes or squares of bright colors. Press down heavily to leave a thick layer of color. Now cover the entire egg with heavy black crayon. Then use a pointed object (perhaps a nail file) to scratch away the black so the color underneath shows through.

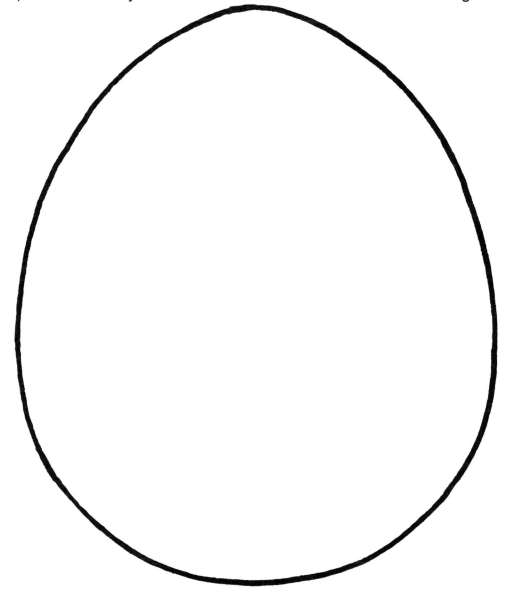

Dates When States Were Admitted to the United States

Alabama	December 14, 1819
Alaska	January 3, 1959
Arizona	February 14, 1912
Arkansas	June 15, 1836
California	September 9, 1850
Colorado	August 1, 1876
Connecticut	January 9, 1788
Delaware	December 7, 1787
Florida	March 3, 1845
Georgia	January 2, 1788
Hawaii	August 21, 1959
Idaho	July 3, 1890
Illinois	December 3, 1818
Indiana	December 11, 1816
Iowa	December 28, 1846
Kansas	January 29, 1861
Kentucky	June 1, 1792
Louisiana	April 30, 1812
Maine	March 15, 1820
Maryland	April 28, 1788
Massachusetts	February 6, 1788
Michigan	January 26, 1837
Minnesota	May 11, 1858
Mississippi	December 10, 1817
Missouri	August 10, 1821
Montana	November 8, 1889
Nebraska	March 1, 1867
Nevada	October 31, 1864
New Hampshire	June 21, 1788
New Jersey	December 18, 1787
New Mexico	January 6, 1912
New York	July 26, 1788
North Carolina	November 21, 1789
North Dakota	November 2, 1889
Ohio	March 1, 1803
Oklahoma	November 16, 1907
Oregon	February 14, 1859
Pennsylvania	December 12, 1787
Rhode Island	May 29, 1790
South Carolina	May 23, 1788
South Dakota	November 2, 1889
Tennessee	June 1, 1796
Texas	December 29, 1845
Utah	January 4, 1896
Vermont	March 4, 1791
Virginia	June 25, 1788
Washington	November 11, 1889
West Virginia	June 20, 1863
Wisconsin	May 29, 1848
Wyoming	July 10, 1890

Dates When Provinces Joined Dominion of Canada

Alberta	September 1, 1905
British Columbia	July 20, 1871
Manitoba	July 15, 1870
New Brunswick	July 1, 1867
Newfoundland	March 31, 1949
Nova Scotia	July 1, 1867
Ontario	July 1, 1867
Prince Edward Island	July 1, 1873
Quebec	July 1, 1867
Saskatchewan	September 1, 1905

Birth Dates of U.S. Presidents

George Washington	February 22, 1732
John Adams	October 30, 1735
Thomas Jefferson	April 13, 1743
James Madison	March 16, 1751
James Monroe	April 28, 1758
John Quincy Adams	July 11, 1767
Andrew Jackson	March 15, 1767
Martin Van Buren	December 5, 1782
William H. Harrison	February 9, 1773
John Tyler	March 29, 1790
James K. Polk	November 2, 1795
Zachary Taylor	November 24, 1784
Millard Fillmore	January 7, 1800
Franklin Pierce	November 23, 1804
James Buchanan	April 23, 1791
Abraham Lincoln	February 12, 1809
Andrew Johnson	December 29, 1808
Ulysses S. Grant	April 27, 1822
Rutherford B. Hayes	October 4, 1822
James A. Garfield	November 19, 1831
Chester A. Arthur	October 5, 1829
Grover Cleveland	March 18, 1837
Benjamin Harrison	August 20, 1833
William McKinley	January 29, 1843
Theodore Roosevelt	October 27, 1858
William H. Taft	September 15, 1857
Woodrow Wilson	December 29, 1856
Warren G. Harding	November 2, 1865
Calvin Coolidge	July 4, 1872
Herbert Hoover	August 10, 1874
Franklin D. Roosevelt	January 30, 1882
Harry S. Truman	May 8, 1884
Dwight D. Eisenhower	October 14, 1890
John F. Kennedy	May 29, 1917
Lyndon B. Johnson	August 27, 1908
Richard M. Nixon	January 9, 1913
Gerald R. Ford	July 14, 1913
Jimmy Carter	October 1, 1924
Ronald Reagan	February 6, 1911

Key to Answers

August

21—The Stilt

23—Gossamer: something light and airy; Condor: bird with huge wings that can fly very high; Albatross: large sea bird whose wings stretch almost 6 feet from tip to tip and can soar for hours. They were light, with large wings for soaring

27—

A	P	K	O	H	R	J	E	S	P	P	B	W	Q
D	D	T	Z	N	S	M	G	D	L	L	F	R	U
E	V	B	K	I	O	U	J	R	S	A	C	E	A
T	I	V	A	C	F	B	K	U	H	S	A	P	R
E	G	A	S	O	L	I	N	E	F	T	G	A	X
R	C	U	P	S	E	R	U	T	N	I	A	P	E
G	L	N	H	L	D	G	X	F	H	C	E	X	O
E	M	Y	A	R	P	S	G	U	B	S	P	A	Y
N	N	Y	L	O	N	M	I	E	J	N	K	W	T
T	W	Y	T	B	O	T	T	L	E	D	G	A	S

29—Foods in order are: baked Alaska; Johnny cake; pralines; hush puppies; sauerbraten; shoo-fly pie; Waldorf salad; tortilla; Brunswick stew; barbecue

September

3—1. $200; 2. $2400; 3. $3750; 4. $3740 per game; 5. $600,000

7—Russia, bear; U.S., Uncle Sam; Republican party, elephant; Canada, maple leaf; Christianity, cross; Democratic party, donkey; Jewish religion, star of David

10—1. tar and crushed stones or concrete; 2. so they could sell more cars; 3. the U.S. government and the states

14—In order, these are anthems of: Federal Republic of Germany; Mexico; Canada; England; Japan; People's Republic of China; Brazil; Italy

17—1. 1941-1950; 2. 1½ million; 3. 20 million; 4. 1961-70; 5. about 6,530,000

20—Please; Thank You; You're Welcome; May I?; I'm Sorry; Hello

21—Yes, We have no bananas!

22—vanilla, chocolate, strawberry; orange, banana, raspberry, butterscotch, butter pecan, walnut

October

2—pile, plea, heal, fog, fig, hog, pig, has, hale, hail, sea, seal, sail, sale, leg, leaf and so on

8—

9—Probably the family would choose the one whose tail is wagging

11—inferior: little or less importance or value; consent; agreeing with the action or opinion

12—1. 1450; 2. 1492; 3. 3 years; 4. 1498; 5. 10 years; 6. 56 years

14—man, first airplane, race horse, antelope, cheetah, automobile, falcon, Boeing 747 jet, Glamorous Glennis, Columbia space shuttle. Supersonic: faster than sound

18—Alabama; 2. last; 3. Atlantic; 4. Southern; 5. Kentucky; 6. America: Alaska

20—

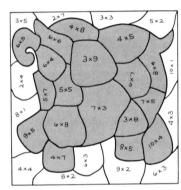

22—3:02; 3:06; 3:13; 3:16; 3:31; 3:32; 3:38

24—With the telegraph, messages could reach the west coast in only a few minutes. Longer messages that were not emergencies could go by stagecoach and railroad

28—1. immigrants; 2. to free someone from ignorance; 3. people thought of New York city as the golden door to the United States

31—

November

2—Answers in order are: migrated, ford, blaze, trail, gap

4—1. shoes; 2. blob; 3. he loses

5—

A	M	W	B	I	U	S	L	R	D	I	T	F	W	S	H
K	C	A	L	B	N	E	L	E	C	T	E	D	U	W	N
Z	J	S	G	I	S	V	A	H	R	K	S	Q	C	A	A
H	S	H	I	R	L	E	Y	C	H	I	S	H	O	L	M
O	V	I	T	C	P	N	R	A	D	O	E	R	U	Y	O
H	T	N	V	G	A	N	F	E	J	M	U	C	N	S	W
L	W	G	K	B	X	W	S	T	A	T	E	V	T	D	C
S	E	T	A	T	S	D	E	T	I	N	U	E	R	L	P
B	G	O	J	F	P	M	S	Q	U	K	D	F	Y	G	E
N	A	N	E	Z	I	T	I	C	M	D	C	O	K	E	H

7—Cars top to bottom at left hold furniture, cattle, truck trailers, oil. Cars at right hold oranges, coal, automobiles, wheat

8—numbers are approximate: 163 B.C.; 86 B.C.; 9 B.C.; A.D. 145; 222; 299; 453; 530; 607; 684; 761; 838; 915; 1069; 1146; 1223; 1300; 1378; 1531; 1607; 1683; 1834; 1910; 1985

12—From top to bottom, definitions explain: necktie, corduroys, T-shirt; jeans; tuxedo; leg warmers; sneakers

17—

18—It is 11:00 in Boston, Toronto, Miami; 10:00 in Des Moines, Dallas, St. Louis; 9:00 in Denver, Phoenix, Calgary; 8:00 in San Francisco, Vancouver, Seattle

19—87 years; the year the Declaration of Independence was signed; when its citizens prosper, a nation grows; to devote it to a real purpose; that the dead did not die without a very good reason; without success; a government in which the people have some part in deciding who governs a country and how it is governed.

25—

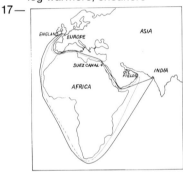

28—84 − 78 + 52 − 2 × 2 + 2000 ÷ 3 − 28 ÷ 2 = 338

30—In the fifth inning, Jets made 2 runs, Rockets made 3 runs.

December

1—Ford, Chevrolet, Mercury, Toyota, Volkswagen, van, pickup truck, tank truck

2—1 plus two Os; three Os; six Os; nine Os; twelve Os; fifteen Os; eighteen Os; twenty-one Os

3—Missing label at left is right atrium. Label at right is left ventricle.

5—quarterback, pigskin, guard, superbowl, touchdown, field goal, forward, goal posts

6—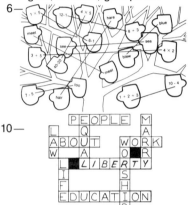

10—

16—Bill's to Gabriele's: east, north, east; Gabriele's to Pedro's: east, south; Pedro's to Manuel's: west; Manuel's to Elise's: west, north; Elise's to home: north, west, north

18—a product or service owned exclusively by one person or one group of people; winning the game usually depends on having all the railroads, or all the utilities, or all the houses on certain streets

20—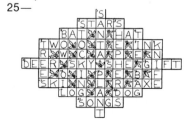

21—magnificent desolation: a strikingly beautiful barren wasteland

22—Products from top to bottom are: cola, spices, ketchup, hamburger, eggs, bread, milk, potatoes

25—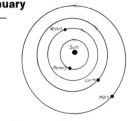

January

3—

7—player on ice skates, hockey; with catcher's mitt, baseball; with tennis racket, tennis; with snorkle, snorkeling; soccer net, soccer; player dribbling football, football

9—He or she fills the balloon with hot air. The balloonist turns off the heater.

11—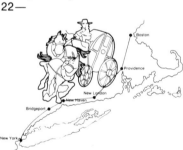

13—Orchestra: A group of musicians, especially those that play string instruments; Conductor: leader of a musical group; Opera: drama set to music; Opera house: theater where operas are performed.

17—bifocal glasses, newspaper, hospital, rocking chair, United States, almanac, harmonica, postal system

22—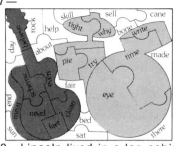

29—Yogi Berra, Fred Clarke, John Clarkson, Ty Cobb, Martin Dihigo, Joe DiMaggio, Cal Hubbard, Carl Hubbell, Judy Johnson, Walter J. Johnson, Mickey Mantle, Christy Mathewson, Babe Ruth, John Peter Wagner, Ted Williams

31—1. Sounds are bounced from earth to satellite to earth, much as an echo; 2. It is used as a transit for navigation; 3. Two; 4. Greek and Roman; 5. Yes, nimbus is a rain cloud; 6. It explored areas of the atmosphere above the earth.

February

3—telephone lineman, auto mechanic, welder, dentist, judge, governor, banker, bus driver

7—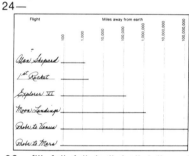

12—Lincoln lived in a log cabin when he was a child.

15—Suffrage: the right of voting; citizen: a person who owes allegiance to a country and can take part in its rights and duties; deny: prevent someone; abridge: limited; enforce: to put this law into action; legislation: laws to put this amendment into action

20—Persons matching definitions from top to bottom are: Douglass, Bethune, Tubman, Truth, Washington, DuBois

23—measles, mumps, polio, small pox, tuberculosis

24—

Flight	Miles away from earth
	100 1,000 10,000 100,000 1,000,000 10,000,000 100,000,000
Alan Shepard	
1st Rocket	
Explorer VI	
Moon Landing	
Probe to Venus	
Probe to Mars	

26—fill, fall, full, bull, ball, lull, and others

29—These are leap years: 1492, 1732, 1776, 1904, 1932, 1984, 2000

March

1—great canyons, deep and interesting caves, large clear blue lake, wood that has turned to stone, large group of sequoia trees, large cave, mountains usually covered with fog to make them look smoky, large glaciers

2—1. odd low no.; 2. even high no.; 3. odd low no.; 1. even high no.; 2. odd low no.; 3. even high no.

9—Possible answers are: Hudson River; America; Colombia, S.A. or Columbus, Ohio; Bering Sea; Straits of Magellan; Vancouver Island, Verrazano Bridge in New York harbor, Cook Is.

11—Blizzard: long, severe snowstorm; tornado: violent and destructive windstorm; hurricane: thunderstorm with winds of 74 miles or higher; tidal wave: unusual rise of water along shore due to strong winds or after an earthquake; earthquake: shaking or trembling of the earth; typhoon: tropical storm with high winds and rain

12—

15—Vulture: 2¼ ft., wing span of 6½ ft.; Condor: 3¾ ft., wing span of 10½ ft.; Eagle: 3 ft., wing span of 7½ ft.; Hawk: 2 ft., wing span of 4½ ft.

17—potatoes, setter, lace, stew, jig, tweed

23—3, 6, 10, 15, 21, 28, 36, 47, 57

24—1. 35; 2. Oct. 2; 3. about 10 miles; 4. about 14½ weeks; 5. over 3 months; 6. 785 miles

27—

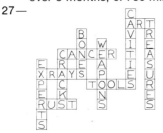

28—subway, submarine, subdivide, substandard, subcompact

31—1. 10:00; 2. early; 3. ahead; 4. In the spring clocks are moved ahead one hour, in the fall they are turned back one hour.

April

6—

7—True answers are 2, 4, 5, 6, 8

8—.336; .241; .320; .244; .180; .292; .285; .250

9—smallest bowlers; very thirsty; very large panda; tiny doll; person who is considered a great baseball player

10—rocking chair, sailboat, stepstool, popcorn, stained glass, clothes line, bookcase, cookbook, bathroom; coffee pot

11—Persons matching definitions from top to bottom are: Wright brothers; Blackwell; Bering; Gagarin; Norsemen; Chisholm; Pike; Armstrong

13—

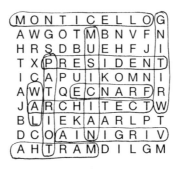

15—1. 24; 2. 1848; 3. 25 qts.; 4. 250 qts.; 5. 62½ gals.; 6. about 115½ gals.

21—

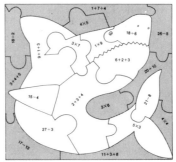

23—gum wrapper, tin can, broken toy, wheel, garbage, tree branch, one mitten, tire, bone, iron rod

28—Italy, Chile, Denmark, Russia, Norway, Japan, Germany, Argentina

30—1. yes; once a person is selected, the person still in office loses interest in his job; 2. the person still in office cannot be a very effective person

May

11—Definitions from top to bottom: Arizona, Kentucky, Michigan, Connecticut, Mississippi, Ohio, Wyoming, Iowa, Nebraska

14—1. 13; 2. 125; 3. 169; 4. 202; 5. 241; 6. 258; 7. 338; 8. 352;

20—signs at left say: stop; no right turn; school crossing. Signs at right say: let cars from other road go first; slow, curving road; railroad crossing

27—Bridges at left are: arch, pontoon, suspension; Bridges at right are: cantilever, truss, simple beam

28—smallmouth bass, largemouth bass, channel catfish, blue gill, yellow perch, rainbow trout, coho salmon, muskellunge, northern pike, bullhead

29—

June

3—

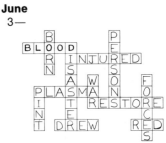

4—

6—

17—

18—

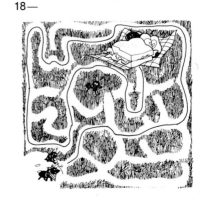